T0135936

Bibliografische Information der Deutschen Nationalbibliothek

Die Deutsche Nationalbibliothek verzeichnet diese Publikation in der Deutschen Nationalbibliografie; detaillierte bibliografische Daten sind im Internet über http://dnb.d-nb.de abrufbar.

ISBN 978-3-8325-3365-6

Logos Verlag Berlin GmbH
Comeniushof, Gubener Str. 47,
10243 Berlin
Tel.: +49 (0)30 42 85 10 90
Fax: +49 (0)30 42 85 10 92
INTERNET: http://www.logos-verlag.de

Department of Informatics
University of Fribourg (Switzerland)

Pretty Good Anonymity

achieving high performance anonymity services with a single node architecture

THESIS

presented to the Faculty of Science of the University of Fribourg (Switzerland) in consideration for the award of the academic grade of *Doctor scientiarum informaticarum*

by
Ronny Standtke
from
Germany

Thesis No: 1771
Logos Verlag Berlin GmbH
2012

Accepted by the Faculty of Science of the University of Fribourg (Switzerland) upon the recommendation of Prof. Dr. Ulrich Ultes-Nitsche, Prof. Dr. Rüdiger Grimm and Prof. Dr. Jacques Pasquier.

Fribourg, 12/12/2012

Thesis supervisor

Prof. Dr. Ulrich Ultes-Nitsche

Dean

Prof. Dr. Rolf Ingold

Jury president

Prof. Dr. Béat Hirsbrunner

Acknowledgements

First of all I want to thank Prof. Dr. Ulrich Ultes-Nitsche, head of the Formal Dependability and Security research group (FDS) at the University of Fribourg for supervising my thesis. I also want to thank my colleagues in the research group, namely Dominik Jungo, David Buchmann, Thierry Nicola, Christoph Ehret, Michael Hayoz, Stephan Krenn, Stefania Barzan, and Carolin Latze for their feedback and suggestions.

Furthermore I would like to thank my colleagues at secunet SwissIT AG for their support and valuable input, namely Dr. Susanne Röhrig, Dr. Lorenz Frey and Dr. Volker Zeuner.

And my biggest thanks go to my wife and my daughters for their endless support and patience through all the time this work has taken.

Abstract

There are several anonymity architectures for Internet communication in use today. They are either unsafe or very complex.

In this work the design, implementation and evaluation of an anonymity architecture that provides a high level of protection and is still simple enough to enable high-bandwidth, low-latency Internet communications is presented.

The architecture uses a single-node anonymity service provider in combination with anonymity groups. The software components of the architecture consist of a client program for end-users, a server program for the anonymity service provider and a remote management component for the server program.

To enable a high-bandwidth and low-latency communication between the client program and the server program a new high-performance IO-framework was designed and implemented.

anonymity, dummy traffic, high performance IO

Zusammenfassung

Verschiedene Verfahren zur Anonymisierung von Internetkommunikation werden heutzutage eingesetzt. Diese Verfahren sind entweder unsicher oder sehr komplex.

In dieser Arbeit wird das Design, die Implementierung und die Evaluation eines Anonymisierungsverfahrens präsentiert, welches einen hohen Schutz bietet und dennoch einfach genug ist, eine breitbandige Internetkommunikation mit niedrigen Latenzzeiten zu ermöglichen.

Das Verfahren verwendet einen nicht-verteilten Anonymisierungsdienst in Kombination mit Anonymitätsgruppen. Die Softwarekomponenten des Verfahrens bestehen aus einem Clientprogramm für Endbenutzer, einem Serverprogramm für den Anonymisierungsdienst und einer Komponente zur Fernwartung des Serverprogramms.

Um eine breitbandige Kommunikation mit geringer Latenzzeit zwischen dem Clientprogramm und dem Serverprogramm zu ermöglichen, wurde ein neues Hochleistungs-I/O-Rahmenwerk entworfen und implementiert.

Anonymität, Dummytraffic, Hochleistungs-I/O

Contents

List of Figures

List of Tables

Chapter 1

Introduction

Anonymity is one of the major goals when aiming at achieving data security — its purpose is confidentiality of communication circumstances (participants, time, duration and data volume of a communication). As with any other security goals, in order to achieve anonymity, there exist various methods to protect oneself against attackers of various strengths: The design and implementation of the anonymity method will depend significantly on the underlying threat model.

For Internet communications, several anonymization techniques have been designed and implemented during the last years. Even within these relatively short time, the attacker model has changed significantly taking into account the increasing monitoring and commercialization of the Internet.

1.1 State of the art

In this section only a very short summary of existing anonymization methods and their corresponding implementations is presented. For a more detailed evaluation see chapter 3.

1.1.1 Proxy

A proxy is a (trustworthy) third party placed in between a user and his/her communications partners. Proxies are well-known components of Internet communications and are available for many protocols. Using a proxy is a very weak anonymization method as an attacker wire-tapping the communication between users and proxy can easily access any information about the current communication by analyzing the address information exchanged between users and proxy.

In summary, anonymization via a proxy is simple but insecure.

1.1.2 Encrypting proxy

The additional feature of an encrypting proxy is that communications between the proxy and its users are encrypted, rendering impossible to reveal communications relations by address evaluation. Encrypting proxies are also well-known and available for many protocols, mostly by adding an SSL-layer [64] above the protocol. But encryption alone does not protect against the many other known attacks on anonymity (see chapter 3) besides address evaluation.

In summary, anonymization via an encrypting proxy is no longer trivial (because of the necessary public key infrastructure needed for secure encryption) but still insecure with respect to anonymization.

1.1.3 Anonymity group

To defend against most known attacks against anonymity, users have to join so-called anonymity groups. Members of an anonymity group must behave identical in many ways (frequency and size of sent and received messages). There are still some attacks against anonymity groups but they are quite sophisticated. Currently, there exists no implementation which solely aims at implementing anonymity groups in a simple and stable way.

In summary, anonymization via anonymity groups is not overly complex, provides a high level of security but lacks an implementation.

1.1.4 Mix

Using anonymity groups, no one can reveal communications relations — except the anonymity provider where the anonymity group is formed. The method of *mixes* [10] tries to exclude, in addition, the possibility of the third party being the attacker. To do so, the third party is partitioned into several so-called mixes and every message will go through all mix instances. A particular coding scheme is used, in which messages are multiply encrypted and decrypted. The additional organizational and technical overhead makes mix implementations very complex. There are still sophisticated attacks against mixes so that the stated goal of protection against the anonymity provider is not completely reached.

In summary, anonymization via mixes provides a high level of security but adds a complex overhead for a questionable gain.

1.2 Motivation

The motivation of this work is the lack of a simple and secure implementation of anonymization via anonymity groups. The goal of this work is to design, implement and evaluate such a solution.

1.2.1 Goals

Here we list the objectives that were set for this work:

Defense against a global attacker: Because one can assume that the global attacker (see section 2.3) will become more and more realistic (or maybe already is), it is the fundamental threat model for this architecture.

Performance: The solution must not collide with current user expectations regarding Internet usage. It must provide users with anonymous, low-latency, high-bandwidth communication links.

Simplicity: The solution's system design must be as simple as possible so that it is easy to understand by developers or code reviewers and straightforward to install and use for both service providers and end users.

Flexibility: The architecture must support TCP-based programs without modification. The architecture should offer multilevel security. This means it must be possible to use the architecture in plain "encrypting proxy" mode if the own security needs are not ranked as high.

1.2.2 Non-goals

Here we list objectives that are explicitly *not* taken into account by this work:

No protocol normalization: If users want anonymity from peers while using protocols that may leak user information (e.g. HTTP) they must layer the solution with a filtering proxy such as Privoxy (`http://www.privoxy.org`[1]). By not filtering protocols, the solution enables users to stay anonymous against the network but still authenticate to a peer.

Not steganographic: The solution has no mechanisms to conceal who is using its services.

[1]last visited: January 2012

Chapter 2

Threat models and countermeasures

The primary goal of anonymization is to protect communication circumstances. At first, we present a simple formal specification of communication circumstances which will be used as the base for further considerations:

In communication there exists a non-empty set of senders X and a non-empty set of recipients Y. The membership between X and Y is undefined, both sets could be identical, be a subset of each other, share intersections or could be completely disjoint. Messages that originate in X and arrive in Y form a graph G with X as the domain and Y as the codomain (see Figure 2.1).

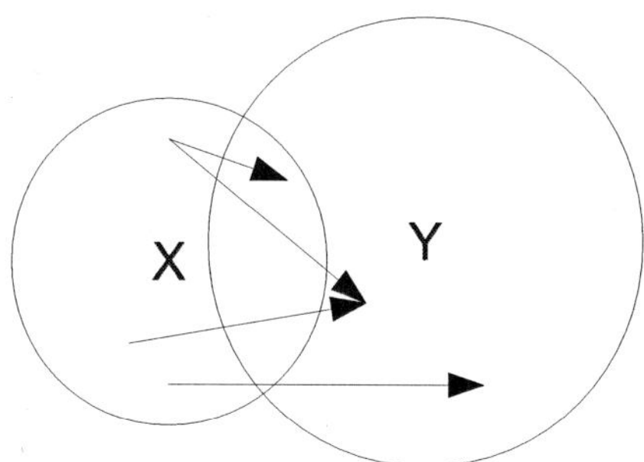

Figure 2.1: sets and graph in communication

Communication circumstances at a certain point in time is the symmetric (and most of the time heterogeneous) binary relation (X, Y, G). An attack against anonymity is therefore defined as gaining knowledge about the communication graph G. There are different threat models against anonymity with different strengths and commonness which are presented in the following sections. They will be evaluated as to their certainty, complexity and existing countermeasures.

2.1 Remote adversary

In this threat model the adversary can only observe Y, i.e. the reception of messages at one or more recipients. When the messages contain sender information (as it is the norm in IP-based communication networks, all packages contain a sender IP), the adversary can gain information about all observed parts of G. Real world examples for adversaries of this threat model are:

- web server operators
- participants in a peer-to-peer communication protocol

This threat model is very weak but probably the most common.

2.1.1 Certainty

The certainty of this attack is absolute.

2.1.2 Complexity

An adversary has to store and evaluate all received messages. Therefore, if n is the number of messages, the complexities of the attack are:

- space: $O(n)$
- time: $O(n)$

2.1.3 Countermeasures

To protect against a remote adversary, a sender must remove the sender information from the messages. In IP-based communication networks, the most straightforward solution is to use a proxy. A proxy is a (trustworthy) third party placed in between a sender and its recipients. During connection establishment, each sender transfers the recipient's address to the proxy by using an appropriate protocol. After the proxy has established a connection to the recipient, it will replace the original sender information with its own information before forwarding messages from the sender to the recipient. The sender remains anonymous as long as it does not reveal its sender information to the recipient in another way (e.g. on a higher level protocol as HTTP where browsers reveal many sender information e. g. via cookies).

2.2 Local adversary

In this threat model the adversary can only observe X, i.e. the sending of messages. When the messages contain recipient information (as it is the norm in IP-based communication networks, all packages contain a destination IP), the adversary can gain information about all observed parts of G.

Real world examples for adversaries of this threat model are:

- intranet operators
- Internet Service Providers

This threat model is very common nowadays.

2.2.1 Certainty

The certainty of this attack is absolute.

2.2.2 Complexity

An adversary has to store and evaluate all sent messages. Therefore, if n is the number of messages, the complexities of the attack are:

- space: $O(n)$
- time: $O(n)$

2.2.3 Countermeasures

To protect against a local adversary, a sender must hide the recipient information in the messages. In IP-based communication networks, senders have to use a proxy but in addition to the basic proxy mechanisms, senders have to encrypt their messages to the proxy. (Actually, only the recipient information must be encrypted to protect anonymity but to also protect the confidentiality of the communication, usually the entire messages are encrypted.) As long as the adversary can not break the message encryption it is impossible for the adversary to gain knowledge about G.

2.3 Global adversary

In this threat model the adversary can observe both X and Y, that means the adversary can observe any message sent and any message received. Considering technical as well as administrative developments in recent years, the potential for this threat model to become reality for the Internet is increasing [16]. From law enforcement authorities to the entertainment industries, various sectors have the need for and technical measures to monitor Internet traffic. Such a powerful adversary can apply various strategies to attack anonymity. Most of these strategies have been mentioned in [40].

2.3.1 Passive Attacks

Passive attacks are executed only by observations and calculations. The adversary does not change any property of the communication infrastructure.

End-to-end content correlation

If the communication graph G has no delay and the adversary can read all messages both in X and Y, the adversary can compare all sent messages with all received messages. The senders and recipients of messages are the vertices and the links between senders and recipients of equal messages form the communication graph G.

In the example given in Figure 2.2 the adversary can observe the following messages:

- sender_1 is sending message s_1 with the contents 'a'
- sender_2 is sending message s_2 with the contents 'b'
- recipient_1 is receiving message r_1 with the contents 'b'
- recipient_2 is receiving message r_2 with the contents 'a'

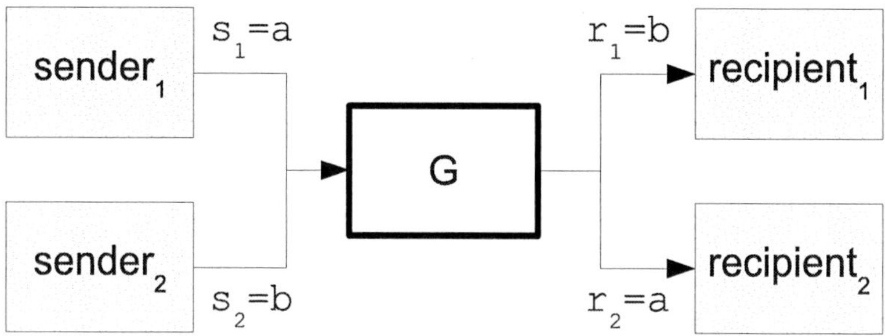

Figure 2.2: end-to-end content correlation example

When x is the index of a sender and y the index of a recipient, attacking the anonymity means to find all index pairs $\{x, y\}$ so that $s_x = r_y$. In the example given above, this would be:

- $\{1, 2\}$
- $\{2, 1\}$

Certainty The certainty of this attack is absolute, as long as the content of all messages in the observation timespan is different.

Complexity An adversary has to store and sort all sent messages of a certain period of time in a collection and store and sort all received messages of the same period of time in another collection. Therefore, if n is the number of messages sent and using an efficient sorting algorithm (e.g. quicksort [27]), the complexities of the attack are:

- space: $O(n)$
- time: $O(n \cdot log(n))$

Countermeasures End-to-end content correlation can be prevented encrypting the messages using probabilistic public key encryption and sending them through a third party in G.

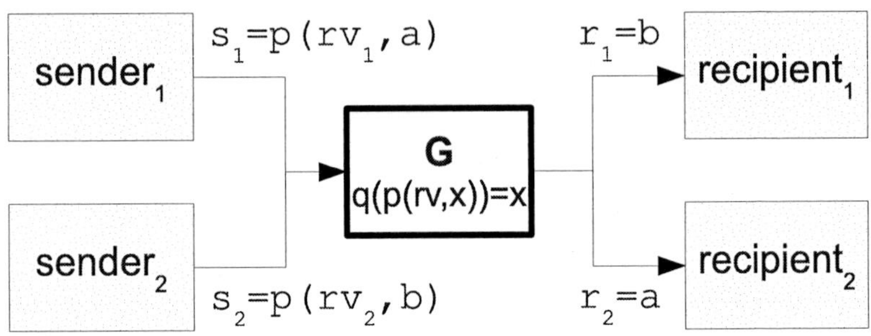

Figure 2.3: end-to-end content correlation prevented by probabilistic public key encryption

In the example given in Figure 2.3 the third party in G has a public key p and a private key q. All senders generate a random value rv_x for every message s_x to send and encrypt it together with the message with p. The third party decrypts these encrypted value pairs with the private key q, discards the random values and forwards the plain text message value r_x to the recipients.

To be able to execute end-to-end content correlation in this case, the adversary must be able to compute $q(p(r, x))$. This is only the case when the adversary has compromised the third party and gained access to the private key q or when the adversary can break the encryption mechanism (which is very unlikely when using only established and well-known mechanisms that have passed the test of time). The encryption mechanism used in this scenario must be secure against adaptive chosen-plain text attacks.

When non-probabilistic public key encryption would be used (no random value would be created and combined with every sent message s_x), the adversary could just compute all $p(r_x)$ of all received messages r_x and use these values for content correlation with all s_x.

End-to-end timing correlation

If the communication graph G has no delay and messages can not be sent simultaneously and the adversary can record all message timestamps both in X and Y, the adversary can compare all timestamps of sent messages with all timestamps of received messages. The senders and recipients of messages are the vertices and the links between senders and recipients of messages with equal timestamps form the communication graph G.

Certainty The certainty of this attack is absolute, as long as the timestamps of all messages are different.

Complexity The attack algorithm and its complexity are similar to the end-to-end content correlation attack. End-to-end timing correlation is probably a little bit more efficient because only short values (timestamps) are stored and sorted instead of large values (message content).

Countermeasures End-to-end timing correlation is impossible to circumvent by one sender alone. Therefore anonymity groups [54] have to be established. An anonymity group is formed by a number of senders. They must send all messages to a third party with the same timing. This way an adversary can no longer correlate message times to a single sender but only to a complete anonymity group. The third party must collect and re-order all messages before forwarding. Otherwise the order of incoming and outgoing messages at the third party would be identical and thus again allow their correlation.

End-to-end data volume correlation

If the communication graph G has no delay and the adversary can record all message sizes both in X and Y, the adversary can compare all sizes of sent messages with all sizes of received messages. The senders and recipients of messages are the vertices and the links between senders and recipients of messages with equal sizes form the communication graph G.

Certainty The certainty of this attack is absolute, as long as the sizes of all messages in the observation timespan are different.

Complexity The attack algorithm and its complexity are similar to the end-to-end timing correlation attack.

Countermeasures End-to-end data volume correlation can only be prevented (as in the previous case of end-to-end timing correlation) by an anonymity group. All anonymity group members must send data at a fixed rate to the third party. If senders have no (meaningful) data to be sent, they must create arbitrary, meaningless traffic (dummy traffic).

Exclusive data volume correlation

If the communication graph G can split but does not inflate messages and the adversary can record all message sizes both in X and Y, the adversary can compare all sizes of sent messages with all sizes of received messages and can exclude that certain received messages have been sent from the same sender when the sum of their sizes is larger than the size of the sent message.

Here is a simple example:

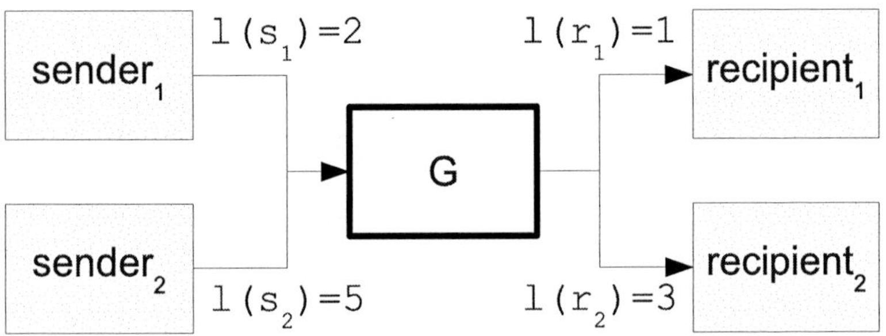

Figure 2.4: exclusive data volume correlation example

At a certain point in time an adversary observes that sender s_1 is sending a message of size 2, sender s_2 is sending a message of size 5, recipient r_1 is receiving a message of size 1 and recipient r_2 is receiving a message of size 3. The adversary then computes all possible size sums of received messages and excludes senders with smaller sent messages:

The remaining possible scenarios in the example above are:

- $s_1 \rightarrow r_1$ and $s_2 \rightarrow r_2$ (both s_1 and s_2 where shortened by G)
- $s_2 \rightarrow r_1$ and $s_2 \rightarrow r_2$ (s_2 was split and shortened by G)

sum	exclusion	reminder
$r_1 = 1$	none	s_1, s_2
$r_2 = 3$	s_1	s_2
$r_1 + r_2 = 4$	s_1	s_2

Table 2.1: Exclusive data volume correlation example

Certainty While the exclusion of certain possible parts of G is absolute, this attack does not directly disclose parts of G. Therefore this attack is only useful to support other types of attack.

Complexity An adversary has to store the sizes of all messages and compute the sum of all possible combinations. Therefore, if n is the number of messages the complexities of the attack are:

- space: $O(n)$
- time: $O(n!)$

The factorial time complexity of this attack makes it very difficult to execute for large numbers of messages.

Countermeasures Exclusive data volume correlation can only be prevented by constructing a communication graph G where messages can be split and shortened. When $l(m)$ is the function that determines the length of a message m, S is the set of sent messages and $R = \{r_1, r_2, ..., r_n\}$ is the set of received messages, the following inequality must be true for G so that no exclusion is possible:

$$\forall s \in S : l(s) > \sum_{i=1}^{n} l(r_n) \tag{2.1}$$

The consequence of this inequality is that the size of sent messages must increase (by adding dummy traffic) with every additional sender who wants to communicate or that the the size of received messages must decrease. Both restrictions result in a degradation of the usable bandwidth for every sender.

Statistical disclosure

If senders send messages only to a limited set of recipients and the sets of senders is not constant and the adversary can record all senders and all recipients of G throughout the time period of the attack, the adversary can gain information about G by statistic evaluation of the recorded data.

To be able to reconstruct the edges of the communication graph G originating from a certain sender, the adversary has to add all distribution sets containing the attacked sender and then subtract all distribution sets not containing the attacked sender.

Here is a simplified example where we assume that the limited set of recipients of each sender is constant:

At the first observation the set of senders consists of $S_1 = \{s_1, s_2\}$ and the set of recipients consists of $R_1 = \{r_1, r_2, r_3\}$. At the second observation the set of senders consists of $S_2 = \{s_1, s_2, s_3\}$ and the set of recipients consists of $R_2 = \{r_1, r_2, r_3, r_4\}$. The communication graph for sender s_3 can be reconstructed by calculating $R_2 - R_1 = \{r_4\}$.

Certainty The certainty of this attack is absolute, as long as the limited set of recipients of each sender is constant, otherwise the certainty of this attack is only probabilistic.

Complexity An adversary has to store all senders and receivers of several observations and has to add and subtract different distribution sets. Therefore, if n is the number of messages and o the number of observations the complexities of the attack are:

- space: $O(n \cdot o)$
- time: $O(n \cdot o)$

Countermeasures Statistical disclosure can only be prevented by disabling the prerequisites of this attack. This can be achieved by using static sets of senders or sending all messages to all recipients and let the recipients decide if a message was meant for them (broadcast and local choice).

In most modern forms of real communications nowadays it is probably unrealistic to assume a static set of senders, users usually join and leave a communication infrastructure very dynamically.

Broadcasting and local choice messages is possible for small communication infrastructures but does not scale very well. For global communication infrastructures like the Internet it is practically impossible.

2.3.2 Active Attacks

Active attacks are executed by changes to communication infrastructure and subsequent observations and calculations.

$n-1$ attack

As described in [33] the adversary isolates one specific sender by simulating all other senders at a certain point in time. As the adversary knows the recipients of all own messages, the set of the victim's recipients can be determined by subtracting the own recipients from the set of all recipients of a certain communication observation.

Certainty The certainty of this attack is absolute.

Complexity Besides the very high social complexity to convince all other senders of a communication infrastructure to cooperate with the adversary, the adversary must store all senders and recipients and subtract sets of observed recipients. Therefore, if n is the number of messages, the complexities of the attack are:

- space: $O(n)$
- time: $O(n)$

Countermeasures $n-1$ attacks can not be prevented by technical measures: The adversary can always try to simulate many other senders or convince other senders to cooperate. Technically speaking, benign senders cannot be distinguished from malicious ones.

2.3.3 Message tampering

If encrypted messages are sent via a third party and an adversary is able to modify or delete these sent messages the adversary can trigger a noticeable change in the set of received messages.

Decrypting a tampered ciphertext without integrity mechanisms (with even only one bit flipped) leads in modern cipher algorithms to a completely random plaintext. This random plaintext can be distinguished from untampered plaintext by measuring the entropy of received messages. Most plaintext messages in todays communication protocols are uncompressed and therefore have a lower entropy than the random plaintext produced by message tampering (see Figure 2.5 for a simple example):

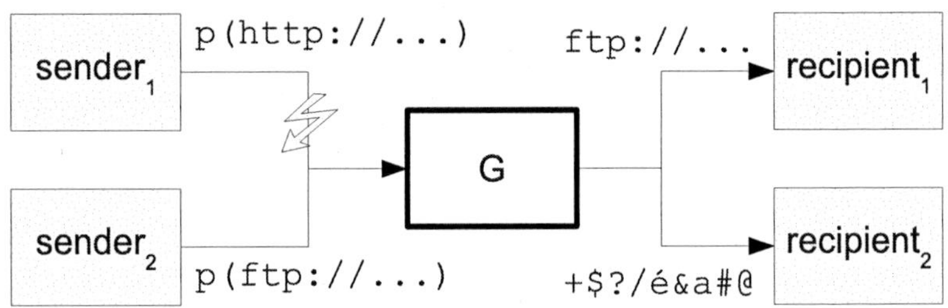

Figure 2.5: message tampering without integrity mechanisms

When the cipher algorithm uses integrity mechanisms to protect against message tampering, the data stream to the recipient does not turn into random white noise as above but just stops. This has the same effect as deleting the sent message and can also easily be detected by a global adversary (see Figure 2.6):

Message tampering can also be used to execute or simplify other attacks:

When executing an $n-1$ attack message tampering can be used to stop all messages of non-cooperating senders. By using message tampering it is no longer necessary to convince all other senders of a communication infrastructure to cooperate with the adversary.

When executing end-to-end correlation attacks, message tampering can be used to destroy sent messages with already observed correlation properties (content, time, size) to make sure that the certainty of the end-to-end correlation attack is absolute (equal correlation properties make the certainty of these attacks only probabilistic).

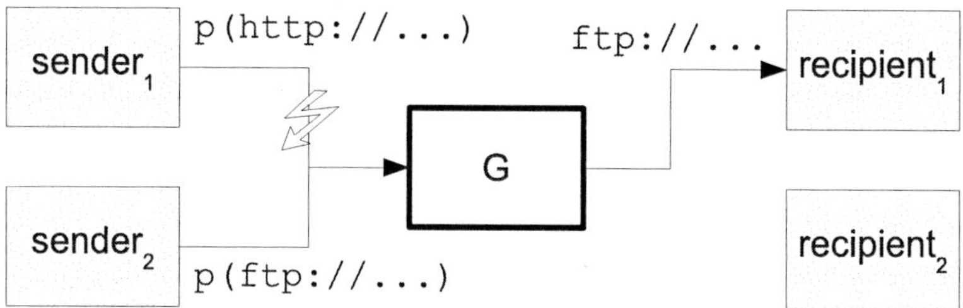

Figure 2.6: message tampering with integrity mechanisms

Certainty The certainty of message tampering without integrity mechanisms is absolute, as long as untampered plaintext messages have a significant lower entropy than completely random messages.

The certainty of message tampering with integrity mechanisms is absolute, as long as G is constant (i.e. no data streams are stopped in normal operation).

Otherwise, the certainty of both attacks is only probabilistic.

Complexity After tampering one message the adversary has to observe all received messages. Therefore, if n is the number of received messages in a certain time frame, the complexities of the attack are:

- space: $O(n)$
- time: $O(n)$

Countermeasures Message tampering attacks can be prevented by using cipher algorithms with integrity mechanisms and only forward messages from the third party to the recipients when an untampered message has been received from all senders. Unfortunately, this countermeasure opens up a new attack vector: an adversary can easily execute a denial-of-service attack by just tampering with a single message of a single sender or by imposing a sender and not sending any message.

2.4 Third party

The most powerful adversary is the (trusted) third party itself. Despite all protection mechanisms at the periphery, the third party must establish a link between users and their peers to enable communication in the end. If the third party can store and correlate all incoming and outgoing messages it can uncover any existing communication association.

Certainty The certainty of this attack is absolute.

Complexity The third party must store the information which outgoing message belongs to which incoming message. Therefore, if n is the number of received messages in a certain time frame, the complexities of the attack are:

- space: $O(n)$
- time: $O(n)$

Countermeasures To protect against the third party itself, the latter must be split up into a distributed system. For the protection mechanisms to be effective, the individual nodes of the distributed system must not cooperate. The ultimate goal is to ensure anonymity even for the case when all nodes but one are compromised.

Because the user data must pass through all involved nodes before it reaches the communication peer, communication via a distributed third party has a relatively high latency and low bandwidth and, in case of commercial offerings where each individual node of the distributed third party charges money for its service, relatively expensive. Additional mechanisms must be established on the user's side to ensure that every part of the distributed system has access only to the particular information it needs. A simple mechanism for that purpose is to use layered encryption (each message is encrypted several times by the user and every node can just decrypt some parts). This idea was first introduced by David Chaum in his seminal paper [10] describing the fundamental building blocks for anonymity.

One option of distributing the third party is to use ad hoc or peer-to-peer [21, 48] networks where any node can join and leave the distributed system anytime. This variant is mostly used by user-driven anonymity services where each user is also partially a trusted third party for other users. There are several disadvantages to this design:

- Latency and bandwidth of the anonymization service are depending on individual user connections, which possibly can be very limited.
- Whenever one node leaves the system, it breaks all the communication links that were routed over this node.
- Volunteers joining the distributed system may be prosecuted for damages done by other (malicious) users of the system. This happened already in Germany where the Public Prosecution Service confiscated anonymization servers of private individuals (e.g. `http://www.golem.de/0609/47702.html`[1]).
- It is not possible in an efficient way to enable all necessary security mechanisms (e.g. dummy traffic) between all distributed nodes, making the system weak against global adversaries.

Another option of third party distribution is to split the third party by organizational means, e.g. by distributing the service to a fixed set of independent organizations. A substantial foundation of this method is the self-obligation of the organizations not to cooperate regarding the de-anonymization of users. The unconditional keeping of this self-obligation cannot be controlled by the users and therefore can be doubted. The whole idea of organizational splitting is inconsistent, because all instances have to collaborate on a technical, organizational and even financial ground just to convince users that exactly these instances do not cooperate.

As stated above, the goal of distributed systems is to ensure the anonymity of the user even against the third party itself. But there are many remaining external attacks, especially *Statistical disclosure* (see section 2.3.1), $n-1$ *attacks* (see section 2.3.2) and *Message tampering* (see section 2.3.3). Protection against the third party only makes sense in the end, if all remaining external attacks are significantly more difficult than internal attacks, which is not the case so far. The attacking third party can just execute an external instead of an internal attack.

In summary, one could say that anonymization over a distributed system is an expensive and even inconsistent method that does not reach its goal. This conclusion is one of the motivations of this work.

[1]last visited: January 2012

Chapter 3

Evaluation of existing solutions

In this chapter the currently available implementations for protecting against different threat models enlisted in chapter 2 are (very shortly) evaluated as presented in [56].

3.1 Proxy

A proxy protects against remote adversaries (see section 2.1).

Proxies are fairly simple programs and exist in different variations, mainly for Internet application-layer protocols. There exist a large number of HTTP and FTP proxies, which are normally placed at the Intranet/Internet border and are accompanied by NAT (Network Address Translation) gateways. Many proxy implementations are Open Source Software and can be categorized as secure and stable. Examples are:

- Web-Proxy Squid (`http://www.squid-cache.org`[1])
- NAT for Linux-Kernel (`http://www.netfilter.org`[2])

Evaluation: Proxies are no solution for anonymous Internet communications because they do not protect against stronger (local and global) adversaries.

[1] last visited: January 2012
[2] last visited: January 2012

3.2 Encrypting Proxy

An encrypting proxy protects against local adversaries (see section 2.2).

Most proxies offer the possibility of encrypted connections. In most cases existing protocols are complemented by the secure sockets layer protocol SSL which takes care of encryption (and mutual user/proxy authentication). As for proxy implementations in general, encrypting proxies are secure and stable. Examples include:

- Anonymizer (`http://www.anonymizer.com`[3])
- Metropipe (`http://www.metropipe.net`[4])
- Proxify (`http://proxify.com`[5])

Evaluation: Encrypting proxies are no solution for anonymous Internet communications because they do not protect against stronger (global) adversaries.

3.3 Mix

The method of using a group of mixes tries to protect against a global adversary including the anonymity provider itself but mostly fails to reach this goal (see section 2.3). There have been several attempts of implementing a mix solution within the last years. Only the most prominent attempts are evaluated in the next sections.

3.3.1 Cypherpunk remailers

A first implementation of a low-bandwidth, high-latency distributed anonymization service was realized in the so-called *cypherpunk remailers* [42]. These remailers offer anonymous e-mail communications and newsgroup postings. At the time of writing, lists of Cypherpunk Remailers can be found here:

- `http://www.noreply.org/echolot/rlist2.html`[6]
- `http://remailer.paranoici.org/rlist.html`[7]

[3] last visited: January 2012
[4] last visited: January 2012
[5] last visited: January 2012
[6] last visited: January 2012
[7] last visited: January 2012

Evaluation: Cypherpunk remailers are no solution for anonymous Internet communications because they provide only low-bandwidth and high-latency communications and do not hide the service its users access (e-mail and newsgroups in this case).

3.3.2 Tor (The Onion Router)

Tor is the second-generation Onion Routing [23, 46, 58, 59, 15] system. It addresses some limitations of the original design but still lacks many security features, making it vulnerable to relatively weak adversaries [40].

Evaluation: The Tor network is no solution for anonymous Internet communications because of its security weaknesses.

3.3.3 JAP (Java Anon Proxy)

JAP [5] was a research project at the Technical University of Dresden (`http://anon.inf.tu-dresden.de`[8], available since September 2001) and uses a mix cascade (fixed sequence of directly linked mixes). Even there, for performance reasons, some important security measures are missing (e.g. dummy traffic). Forced by German police authorities the JAP project integrated a surveillance function into the mix implementation without immediately informing its users (see `http://www.heise.de/newsticker/data/uma-18.08.03-001/`[9]). For many users that action was a betrayal of trust and the most serious set-back for the project. The surveillance function remained in JAP and can still be activated for any addresses. This way, JAP no longer complies with the original goal - to protect the users against the mix operators.

Evaluation: JAP is no solution for anonymous Internet communications because of its high technical and organizational complexity and non-compliance with its own goals.

[8]last visited: January 2012

[9]last visited: January 2012

Chapter 4

Design of PGA

The above evaluation of threat models, countermeasures and their implementations led to this work, called *PGA* (Pretty Good Anonymity).

The evaluation of the third party adversary threat model done in section 2.4 has demonstrated that the efforts needed for a distributed anonymity service provide only a questionable security gain.

In addition to all theoretical and technical considerations how secure anonymous architectures can be build, a balance with past experiences and current politics had to be found. Prof. Dr. Andreas Pfitzmann, leading the JAP research project, disclosed in an interview (see `https://www.datenschutzzentrum.de/interviews/pfitzmann/`[1]) that they where considering to switch off JAP because child abuses where prepared via JAP and only the build-in surveillance function (see `http://anon.inf.tu-dresden.de/dataretention_en.html`[2]) let them continue with the project. Current politics make it very unlikely that an anonymity service without a data retention module can even be legally operated (see current EU directive on data retention [16]). All considerations above lead to the decision to design PGA as a single-node anonymity service, very similar to a single mix instance.

A software developing process is (or more realistically: should) usually put in place when developing a software product, including activities like planning, implementation, testing, documenting, verification, integration, deployment, training, support and maintenance. Several models to organize these activities exist, e.g. the waterfall model [52], spiral model [7], agile development [4] or iterative and

[1]last visited: January 2012

[2]last visited: January 2012

incremental development model [35].

As a research project, the software development process of PGA was rather simple and consisted only of the activities of planning, implementation, testing and documentation. The activities where organized closely to the iterative and incremental development model.

The syntax specified in this document is described in both prose and an augmented Backus-Naur Form [34]. The US-ASCII coded character set is defined by ANSI X3.4-1986 [1]. The following rules are used throughout this document:

```
OCTET         = <any 8-bit sequence of data>
CR            = <US-ASCII CR, carriage return (13)>
LF            = <US-ASCII LF, linefeed (10)>
CRLF          = CR LF
SP            = <US-ASCII SP, space (32)>
DIGIT         = <any US-ASCII digit "0".."9">
UPALPHA       = <any US-ASCII uppercase letter "A".."Z">
LOALPHA       = <any US-ASCII lowercase letter "a".."z">
ALPHA         = UPALPHA | LOALPHA
HEX           = "A" | "B" | "C" | "D" | "E" | "F" |
                "a" | "b" | "c" | "d" | "e" | "f" | DIGIT
```

4.1 Overview

The PGA architecture is divided into two main components, the local proxy (PGA Client) and the server component (PGA Server). The PGA Client has to be installed within the trusted zone of every user, the PGA Server at the provider of the anonymization service. The PGA Server is divided into a core and a remote management front end (see Figure 4.1). Fore secure authentication when establishing connections to the PGA Server, all components have to interact with a CA (Certificate Authority) for certificate management.

Two protocols had to be designed and implemented:

The PGA tunnel protocol is the protocol for exchanging data between the PGA Client and the PGA Server and includes services like logging in, joining or leaving an anonymity group, opening and closing connections to communica-

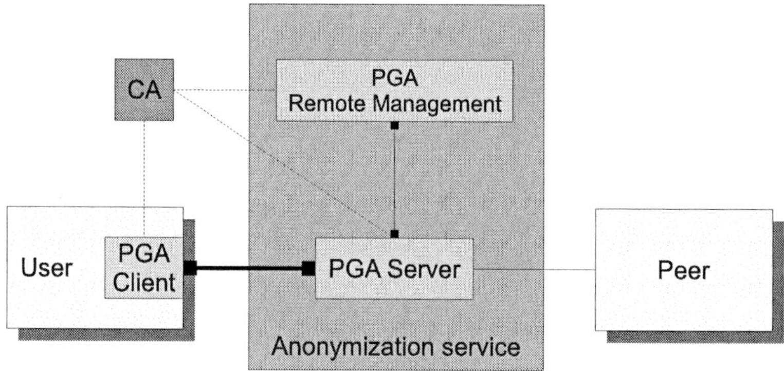

Figure 4.1: PGA overview

tion peers, exchanging status information, etc. More information about this protocol is given in section 4.6.

The PGA remote management protocol is the protocol for exchanging data between the PGA Remote Management and the PGA Server and includes services like starting or stopping the PGA Server, management of anonymity groups, certificates, data volumes, logging, statistics, etc. More information about this protocol is given in section 4.7.

4.2 Client

The requirements for the PGA Client, defined by the author of this work, are as follows:

Platform independence The PGA Client should be usable on the widest range of devices that have Internet connectivity (desktops, laptops, tablet computers, smartphones, ...) and should be compatible with the widest range of operating systems currently in use.

Application independence As many applications as possible must be able to communicate via PGA. Besides the higher value of the PGA architecture to the end user, this requirement also improves the security of the PGA architecture because in contrast to e.g. cypherpunk remailers, it no longer reveals to an adversary the services utilized by its users.

Simplicity For end-users the PGA Client should be easy to install and to use. For reviewers and developers the PGA Client source code must be easy to understand and evaluate. The basic idea behind this requirement is that the larger the group of people reviewing the PGA Client source code is, the simpler it is to establish a reasonable level of trust in the safety of the PGA Client.

Multilevel Security Users must be able to decide if they want to go to the time and effort of full anonymization by joining an anonymity group or if using the PGA Server as a simple encrypting proxy is enough.

4.2.1 Achieving platform independence

To satisfy the requirement of platform independence, the PGA Client was implemented in the programming language Java [24]. Programs implemented in Java run on every platform where a Java Virtual Machine [37] is available. At the time of writing this consists of almost all hardware platforms with Internet connectivity and their operating systems.

The graphical user interface is completely separated from the core (see Figure 4.2). This way it becomes possible to implement different graphical user interfaces for devices with different form factors (everything between e.g. desktop systems with large monitors, smartphones with small screens and embedded systems with only a one-line seven-segment display).

The graphical user interface is based on the interface `HandshakeCompleted-Listener` (which is part of the Java NIO framework, see chapter 5 on page 107) and the abstract class `PgaClientUI` (see Figure 4.3).

The interface `HandshakeCompletedListener` has the following methods:

`handshakeCompleted(sslSession:SSLSession)` is invoked on registered objects when an SSL handshake is completed. This method is used in the PGA Client UI to extract and show information about the cipher suite (protocol, asymmetric cipher, symmetric cipher, hash function) that was selected as the result of the SSL handshake process between the PGA Client and the PGA Server when establishing a tunnel connection.

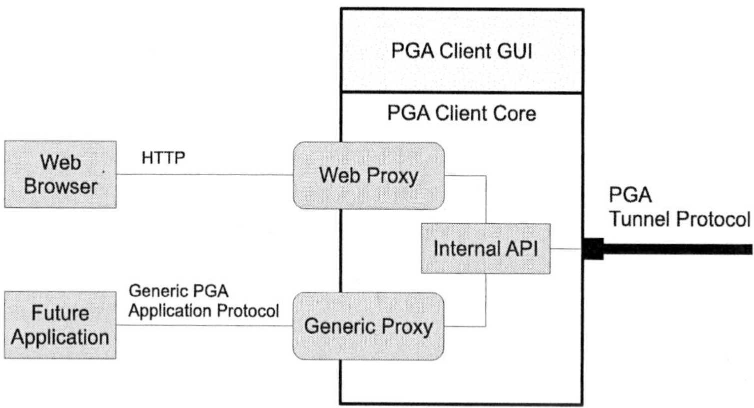

Figure 4.2: PGA Client overview

The abstract class `PgaClientUI` has the following methods:

`connectionSucceeded()` is invoked when the connection to a PGA Server was successfully established.

`connectionCanceled()` is invoked when the user canceled establishing the connection to a PGA Server.

`connectionFailed(errorMessage:String)` is invoked when establishing the connection to a PGA Server failed. The parameter `errorMessage` contains a message with a detailed error description.

`connectionLost()` is invoked when an established connection to a PGA Server broke down.

`setStaticServerState(staticServerState:StaticServerState)` is called after a connection to a PGA Server was established and the PGA Server transferred its initial static state information (see definition of class `StaticServerState` below).

`setDynamicServerState(dynamicServerState:DynamicServerState)` is called every time the PGA Server sends a dynamic state update (see definition of class `DynamicServerState` below).

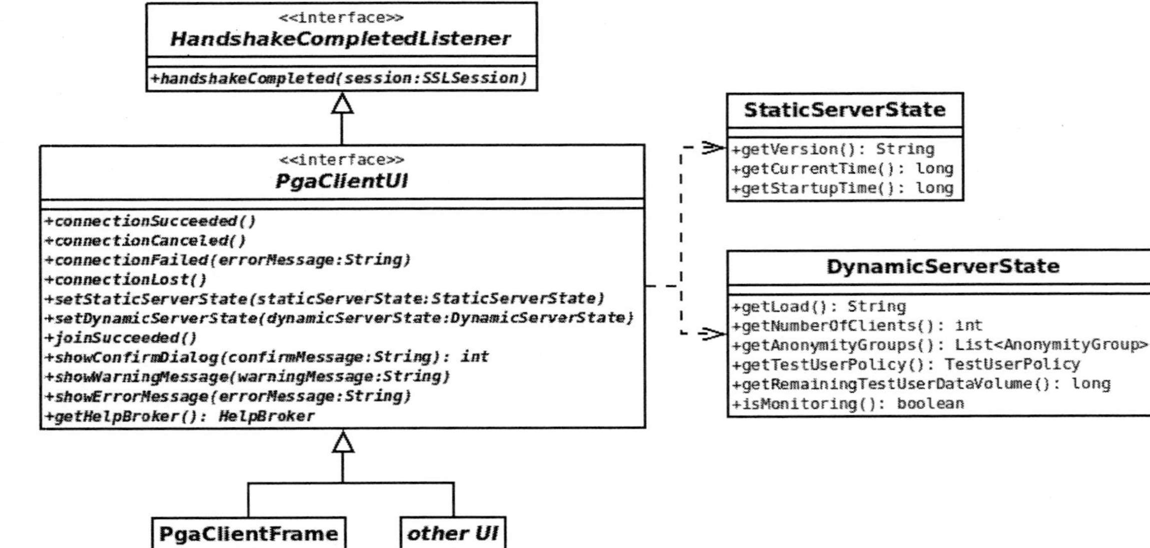

Figure 4.3: PGA Client UI class diagram

`joinSucceeded()` is called when the PGA Client successfully joined an anonymity group.

`showConfirmDialog(confirmMessage:String):int` can be used to show the user a confirmation dialog with the message `confirmMessage`. This method returns the option that was selected by the user (`OK`, `Cancel`, `Close`, ...).

`showWarningMessage(warningMessage:String)` can be used tho show the user a warning message.

`showErrorMessage(errorMessage:String)` can be used to show the user an error message.

`getHelpBroker():HelpBroker` returns a help broker that can be used to present a section of the PGA Client user manual in the user interface.

The class `StaticServerState` has the following methods:

`getVersion():String` returns the version of the PGA Server Core. The version information is used to decide if the selected PGA Server is compatible with the PGA Client currently in use.

`getCurrentTime():long` returns the current time of the PGA Server Core, given in milliseconds since midnight, January 1, 1970 UTC. This time is used to calculate the time offset between the selected PGA Server Core and the PGA Client.

`getStartupTime():long` returns the startup time of the PGA Server Core, given in milliseconds since midnight, January 1, 1970 UTC. This time, together with the calculated time offset (see above) is used to show the uptime of the selected PGA Server Core at regular time intervals in the PGA Client user interface.

The class `DynamicServerState` has the following methods:

`getLoad():String` returns a textural representation of the load of the PGA Server Core. The syntax and semantic of the load information depends on the operation system of the PGA Server Core.

`getNumberOfClients():int` returns the current number of PGA Clients connected to the PGA Server Core.

`getAnonymityGroups():List<AnonymityGroup>` returns the list of all anonymity groups the PGA Server Core currently supports.

`getTestUserPolicy():TestUserPolicy` returns the current policy of the PGA Server Core regarding anonymous users (see section 4.4.1 on page 63).

`getRemainingTestUserDataVolume():long` returns the remaining data volume that is available for anonymous users.

`isMonitoring():boolean` returns `true`, if the PGA Server Core is monitoring connections, `false` otherwise. This is part of the misuse discouragement feature of the PGA Server Core (see section 4.4.1 on page 64).

Currently, there is only one UI implemented, `PgaClientFrame`, a Swing [29] based GUI for usual desktop or laptop screen sizes. It implements all methods of the interface `HandshakeCompletedListener` and the abstract class `PgaClientUI` (for readability reasons the implementation of methods in `PgaClientFrame` is not shown in Figure 4.3). Other user interfaces for other device classes can be implemented in the same way.

4.2.2 Achieving application independence

Overview

To satisfy the requirement of application independence, already existing applications should be able to communicate via PGA without any modification. This goal can be reached by offering plug-ins in the PGA Client for different existing applications and protocols. Future applications that aim at directly supporting PGA must be supported with an easy to use and generic interface (see Figure 4.2).

Plug-In architecture

The plug-in architecture is based on an abstract class `Connector` (see Figure 4.4).

It has the following attributes:

`name` is the descriptive and human-readable name of this Connector.

`icon` is the icon of this Connector presented to the user in the PGA Client graphical user interface.

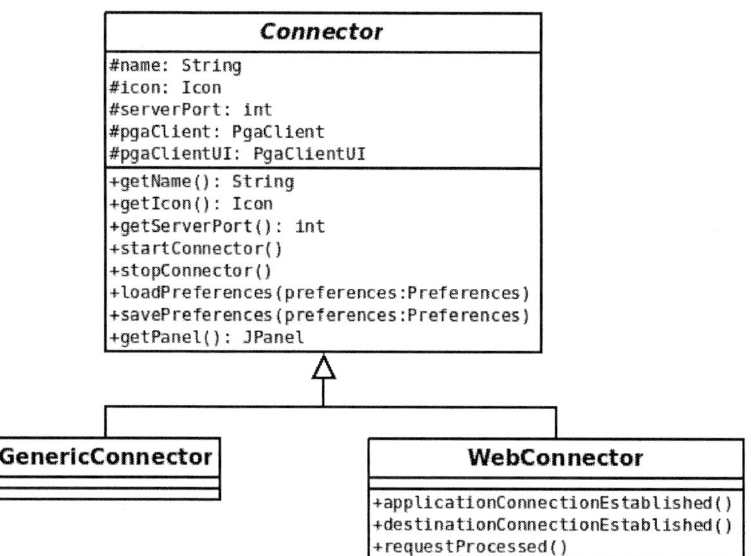

Figure 4.4: Connector class diagram

`serverPort` is the port where this Connector accepts new connections from applications.

`pgaClient` is a reference to the PGA Client Core and is mainly used to always get an up-to-date reference to the tunnel to the currently selected PGA Server.

`pgaClientUI` is a reference to the graphical user interface currently in use. It is mainly used to display status and error messages of the Connector at the graphical user interface.

The abstract class `Connector` has the following methods:

`getName()` returns the descriptive and human-readable name of this Connector.

`getIcon()` returns the icon of this Connector presented to the user in the PGA Client graphical user interface.

`getServerPort()` returns the port where this Connector accepts new connections from applications.

`startConnector()` starts the Connector so that it accepts connections from applications at the specified server port.

`stopConnector()` stops the Connector so that it no longer accepts connections from applications at the specified server port.

`loadPreferences(preferences:Preferences)` loads the preferences of this Connector from a given hierarchical collection of preference data[3].

`savePreferences(preferences:Preferences)` saves the preferences of this Connector into a given hierarchical collection of preference data.

`getPanel()` returns a graphical panel for the graphical user interface currently in use with controls for configuring this Connector.

All plug-ins must implement the abstract class `Connector`. Until now two plug-ins have been designed and implemented:

[3]In most cases this will be the preferences collection of the whole PGA Client.

`GenericConnector` This plug-in offers an easy interface for future applications that aim at directly supporting PGA. When accepting a TCP [9] connection from an application, this plug-in uses the following protocol:

1. Addressing

   The application transmits the host name and port number of the communication peer in one line, delimited by a line feed:

   ```
   address    = hostname ":" portnumber LF
   hostname   = <any OCTET except LF and ":">
   portnumber = 1*DIGIT
   ```

2. Connection establishment

   The GenericConnector tries to open an anonymous connection to the specified location and transmits the status back to the application. The syntax of this status message is defined as follows:

   ```
   status        = success | failure
   success       = LF
   failure       = error-message
                   LF
   error-message = <any OCTET except LF>
   ```

   In other words, when the connection was successfully established, the GenericConnector sends a single line feed to the application, otherwise (e.g. when there is no connection to a PGA Server or an external error like a refused connection on the peer side or a non-existing peer) it sends a human readable error message that is delimited by a line feed.

3. Data exchange

   If the connection was successfully established the data exchange can start. The data depends solely on the application and the communication peer. The PGA infrastructure does not parse or modify the data in any way but forwarding it in a bidirectional tunnel.

4. Connection closing

   TCP connections are bidirectional and can be closed asynchronously from either side, the application or the communication peer.

`WebConnector` This plug-in implements a proxy for HTTP [17] and this way enables most WWW [50] applications to anonymize communication via PGA. The details of this plug-in are described in section 4.3.

The `WebConnector` has the following additional methods that are mainly used for collecting statistics about HTTP requests served with this plug-in:

`applicationConnectionEstablished()` gets called when an application (e.g. a web browser) has successfully established a connection to this plug-in.

`destinationConnectionEstablished()` gets called when a connection to a specified destination (e.g. a web server) has been successfully established.

`requestProcessed()` gets called when a single HTTP request (e.g. HEAD or GET) was successfully served.

4.2.3 Achieving simplicity

Installation

One of the simplest ways to install Java-based applications currently available is Java Web Start. A quote from `http://www.java.com/en/download/faq/java_webstart.xml`[4]:

> The Java Web Start software allows you to download and run Java applications from the web. The Java Web Start software:
>
> - Provides an easy, one-click activation of applications
> - Guarantees that you are always running the latest version of the application
> - Eliminates complicated installation or upgrade procedures

Because of these properties, the installation of the PGA Client is done via Java Web Start.

[4]last visited: January 2012

Usage

To make the usage of the PGA Client as simple as possible, all necessary operations are supported by its graphical user interface. Additional features besides all necessary security mechanisms to be implemented are:

AutoStart is a feature that enables the PGA Client to start automatically whenever a user logs into the system and this way relieves the user from the burden of manually starting the PGA Client at every login. This feature is not only there for convenience but in addition improves the security of the user because it lowers the probability of non-anonymous communication by accident because the user did not start the PGA Client in time.

AutoProxy is a feature that reconfigures common applications automatically so that these applications communicate via PGA. This requirement resulted from the observation that seemingly simple tasks like changing the proxy configuration of a web browser is too challenging for the average user.

Evaluation

To make source code reviews and evaluations of the PGA Client as simple as possible, several measures have to be taken:

Source code readability can be ensured by:

- using a meaningful variable naming scheme (e.g. using descriptive names instead of single letters)
- following established code conventions (see "Code Conventions for the Java Programming Language" currently published at `http://www.oracle.com/technetwork/java/codeconv-138413.html`[5])
- ensuring an overall consistency in the source code by not using different schemes or conventions

Source code documentation must be provided so that the API documentation of the PGA Client can be generated in a more accessible format (e.g. HTML) than the source code itself.

[5] last visited: January 2012

Code reuse of existing and well-known Open Source programming libraries must be the preferred way of implementing a feature so that the amount of code to be reviewed is minimized. Closed Source libraries must not be used in the PGA Client because reviewing or evaluating these libraries is difficult or sometimes even impossible.

4.3 HTTP proxy

The HTTP proxy implemented in the WebConnector plug-in must translate between HTTP and the internal PGA tunnel protocol (see section 4.6). It must parse proxy requests of HTTP client applications and the corresponding HTTP responses. For performance reasons it must support persistent proxy connections with HTTP client applications and manage the creation and shutdown of single connections to HTTP servers.

The syntax of a generic HTTP message is as follows:

```
generic-message = start-line
                  *(message-header CRLF)
                  CRLF
                  [ message-body ]
```

In previous versions of HTTP the normal situation was to establish a TCP connection from the client to the server (or the proxy), send a message and close the TCP/IP connection as soon as the body of the message was fully transmitted. Proxies could just parse the message header (which is a relatively slow operation) and as soon as the message body started, proxies could switch to a very efficient data transfer mode where the transmitted data was no longer parsed. The problem of this modus operandi is the increased computational overhead and latency when requesting several entities from the same server (e.g. a web page and all its embedded pictures) because several slow operations when opening a TCP connection (handshake, slow start, etc.) must be executed every time for every single request.

Therefore HTTP/1.1 defined persistent connections between the application (e.g. web browser) and the server or the proxy. This way several requests (in the case of a proxy-connection even to completely different servers) and responses can be exchanged via the same TCP/IP connection. The additional difficulty is now to decide when a message body has been fully transmitted and the next message header has to be parsed.

Because of the above reasons the PGA Client HTTP proxy has to parse all requests and responses and establish the requested connections to the target servers through the PGA architecture. Another reason are the so-called "hop to hop" protocol headers of HTTP. These headers are part of HTTP and contain administrative information meant only for the next hop of a HTTP connection and must be removed by the hop. Proxies are such next hops.

To be able to parse HTTP requests and responses the syntax and semantic of HTTP, which is described in detail in RFC 2616 [18] (which is 176 pages long), has to be fully understood. In the following paragraphs the structure, syntax and semantic of HTTP proxy requests and responses is shortly analyzed to solve the question how to translate between HTTP and the PGA tunnel protocol.

4.3.1 Request Parsing

A request is a special HTTP message with the following syntax:

```
Request = Request-Line
          *((general-header |
             request-header |
             entity-header) CRLF)
          CRLF
          [ message-body ]
```

Request line

The request line has the following syntax:

```
Request-Line = Method SP Request-URI SP HTTP-Version CRLF
```

HTTP/1.1 specifies a list of methods that can occur in a `Request-Line`:

```
Method = OPTIONS | GET | HEAD | POST | PUT | DELETE | TRACE | CONNECT
```

A short investigation has shown that the methods `HEAD`, `GET` (requesting data from a server), `POST` (sending data to a server) and `CONNECT` (establishing a transparent connection to a server, used for HTTPS via a proxy) are sufficient for supporting basic WWW access of current web browsers. Due to time constraints the HTTP proxy of the PGA Client will only implement these methods. The HTTP proxy will answer all other requests with the status code 501 ("Not Implemented").

The `Request-URI` in a `Request-Line` is a Uniform Resource Identifier and identifies the resource upon which to apply the request and has the following definition:

```
Request-URI = "*" | absoluteURI | abs_path | authority
```

The four possible values of a `Request-URI` are dependent on the nature of the request.

`"*"` means that the request does not apply to a particular resource, but to the server itself, and is only allowed when the method used does not necessarily apply to a resource.

`absoluteURI` is required when the request is, like in this case of the PGA Client HTTP proxy, being made to a proxy. An example `Request-Line` would be:

```
GET http://www.w3.org/pub/WWW/TheProject.html HTTP/1.1
```

After receiving such a request the PGA Client HTTP proxy must:

1. extract the address of the HTTP server from the request
2. translate the request into an internal API call of the PGA Client to establish an anonymous connection to the HTTP server
3. translate the proxy request into a standard HTTP request
4. forward the standard HTTP request and the request body to the HTTP server
5. parse and forward the response from the HTTP server back to the HTTP client
6. manage the shutdown of the connection to the HTTP client and HTTP server

`abs_path` is a `Request-URI` that is used to identify a resource on a server. In this case the absolute path of the URI must be transmitted as the `Request-URI` and the network location of the URI (authority) must be transmitted in an additional `Host` header field. For example, a client wishing to retrieve the resource above directly from the origin server (instead of using a proxy) would create a TCP connection to port 80 of the host `www.w3.org` and transmit these lines:

```
GET /pub/WWW/TheProject.html HTTP/1.1
Host: www.w3.org
```

followed by the remainder of the `Request`.

`authority` is a `Request-URI` that is only used by the `CONNECT` method and specifies the target system of the SSL tunnel that has to be established by the PGA Client HTTP proxy.

Headers

A HTTP request can contain several blocks with `headers` after the `Request-Line` (see HTTP request definition on page 39).

There exist two categories of HTTP headers:

end-to-end headers are transmitted to the ultimate recipient of a request or response

hop-by-hop headers are meaningful only for a single transport-level connection, and are not passed through by proxies

General Headers

General headers have applicability for both request and response messages. HTTP/1.1 defines the following set of general header fields:

```
general-header = Cache-Control | Connection | Date | Pragma |
                 Trailer | Transfer-Encoding | Upgrade |
                 Via | Warning
```

The following paragraphs explain how these headers are used by the PGA Client HTTP Proxy.

`Cache-Control` is an end-to-end header that is used to specify directives that must be obeyed by all caching mechanisms along the request/response chain. This header is ignored by the PGA Client HTTP proxy, since it is not (yet) a caching proxy, and must be passed through.

`Connection` is a hop-by-hop header and allows the sender to specify options that are desired for that particular transport-level connection. The PGA Client HTTP proxy must parse this header and remove it from the message. Persistent connections are the default behavior with HTTP/1.1 but if a

```
Connection: close
```

header is received, the PGA Client HTTP proxy must close the transport-level connection to the application after completing the HTTP response.

`Date` is an end-to-end header that represents the date and time at which a HTTP message was originated. The PGA Client HTTP proxy does not need to parse this header and must pass it through.

`Pragma` is an end-to-end header that is used to include implementation-specific directives that might apply to any recipient along the request/response chain. The PGA Client HTTP proxy does not need to parse this header and must pass it through.

`Trailer` is a hop-by-hop header and its value indicates that the given set of header fields is present in the trailer of a message encoded with chunked transfer-coding. The PGA Client HTTP proxy must parse this header and remove it from the message.

`Transfer-Encoding` is a hop-by-hop header and indicates what (if any) type of transformation has been applied to the message body in order to safely transfer it between the sender and the recipient. Because the PGA Client HTTP proxy does not change the encoding of a message body but just transparently forwards it, the PGA Client HTTP proxy must pass this header through, even though it is a hop-by-hop header.

`Upgrade` is a hop-by-hop header and allows the client to specify what additional communication protocols it supports and would like to use if the server (in this case the PGA Client HTTP proxy) finds it appropriate to switch protocols. The PGA Client HTTP proxy ignores this header and must remove it from the message.

`Via` is an end-to-end header that must be inserted by the PGA Client HTTP proxy to indicate the intermediate protocols and recipients between the applications and the server on requests, and between the server and the applications on responses. It should contain the HTTP version of the received message and a fixed pseudonym of the PGA Client HTTP proxy.

`Warning` is an end-to-end header that is used to carry additional information about the status or transformation of a message which might not be reflected in the message. The PGA Client HTTP proxy does not need to parse this header and must pass it through.

Request Headers

Request headers can only be applied to HTTP requests. HTTP/1.1 defines the following set of request headers:

```
request-header = Accept | Accept-Charset | Accept-Encoding |
                 Accept-Language | Authorization | Expect | From |
                 Host | If-Match | If-Modified-Since |
                 If-None-Match | If-Range | If-Unmodified-Since |
                 Max-Forwards | Proxy-Authorization | Range |
                 Referer | TE | User-Agent
```

In addition to the HTTP/1.1 specification, some HTTP agents use the non-standard header `Proxy-Connection` (see `http://www.http-stats.com/Proxy-Connection`[6]) or the *response*-header field `Keep-Alive` (see `http://www.http-stats.com/Keep-Alive`[7]).

`Accept` is an end-to-end header that is used to specify certain media types which are acceptable for the response. The PGA Client HTTP proxy does not need to parse this header and must pass it through.

[6] last visited: January 2012

[7] last visited: January 2012

`Accept-Charset` is an end-to-end header that is used to indicate what character sets are acceptable for the response. The PGA Client HTTP proxy does not need to parse this header and must pass it through.

`Accept-Encoding` is an end-to-end header that is used to indicate what content-codings are acceptable in the response. The PGA Client HTTP proxy does not need to parse this header and must pass it through.

`Accept-Language` is an end-to-end header that is used to indicate what set of natural languages that are preferred as a response to the request. The PGA Client HTTP proxy does not need to parse this header and must pass it through.

`Authorization` is an end-to-end header that is used to indicate that a user agent wishes to authenticate at a server. The PGA Client HTTP proxy does not need to parse this header and must pass it through.

`Expect` is an end-to-end header that is used to indicate that particular server behaviors are required by the client. The PGA Client HTTP proxy does not need to parse this header and must pass it through.

`From` is an end-to-end header that, if given, should contain an Internet e-mail address for the human user who controls the requesting user agent. Even though this header is contrary to all anonymization efforts, the PGA Client HTTP proxy does not parse or remove this header but passes it through. A user might have valid reasons to use an anonymization service but still disclose the user's identity to the server. This design decision is consistent with the non-goals of the PGA project declared in section 1.2.2 on page 3, i.e. *no protocol normalization*.

`Host` is an end-to-end header that is used to specify the Internet host and port number of the resource being requested. The PGA Client HTTP proxy will probably never receive this header in a request, does not need to parse it and must pass it through.

`If-Match` is an end-to-end header that is used with a method to make it conditional. A client that has one or more entities previously obtained from the resource can verify that one of those entities is current by including a list of their associated entity tags in this header. The PGA Client HTTP proxy does not need to parse this header and must pass it through.

`If-Modified-Since` is an end-to-end header that is used with a method to make it conditional. If the requested variant has not been modified since the time specified in this header, an entity will not be returned from the server; instead, a 304 (not modified) response will be returned without any message-body. The PGA Client HTTP proxy does not need to parse this header and must pass it through.

`If-None-Match` is an end-to-end header that is used with a method to make it conditional. A client that has one or more entities previously obtained from the resource can verify that none of those entities is current by including a list of their associated entity tags in this header. The PGA Client HTTP proxy does not need to parse this header and must pass it through.

`If-Range` is an end-to-end header that is used with a method to make it conditional. If a client has a partial copy of an entity in its cache, and wishes to have an up-to-date copy of the entire entity in its cache, it could use the `Range` request-header with a conditional `GET` (using either or both of `If-Unmodified-Since` and `If-Match`.) However, if the condition fails because the entity has been modified, the client would then have to make a second request to obtain the entire current entity-body. The `If-Range` header allows a client to "short-circuit" the second request. Informally, its meaning is "if the entity is unchanged, send me the part(s) that I am missing; otherwise, send me the entire new entity". The PGA Client HTTP proxy does not need to parse this header and must pass it through.

`If-Unmodified-Since` is an end-to-end header that is used with a method to make it conditional. If the requested resource has not been modified since the time specified in this field, the server should perform the requested operation as if the `If-Unmodified-Since` header were not present. If the requested variant has been modified since the specified time, the server must not perform the requested operation, and must return a 412 (Precondition Failed). The PGA Client HTTP proxy does not need to parse this header and must pass it through.

`Max-Forwards` is an end-to-end header that provides a mechanism with the `TRACE` and `OPTIONS` methods to limit the number of proxies or gateways that can forward the request to the next inbound server. Because in its current form the PGA Client HTTP proxy only implements the `HEAD`, `GET` and `POST` methods, it ignores this header and removes it from the message.

`Proxy-Authorization` is a hop-by-hop header that allows the client to identify itself (or its user) to a proxy which requires authentication. Because the PGA Client HTTP proxy does not have any authorization mechanisms, it ignores this header.

`Range` is an end-to-end header that is used in HTTP retrieval requests using conditional or unconditional `GET` methods to request one or more sub-ranges of the entity, instead of the entire entity. The PGA Client HTTP proxy does not need to parse this header and must pass it through.

`Referer`[8] is an end-to-end header that allows the client to specify, for the server's benefit, the address (URI) of the resource from which the Request-URI was obtained. Similar to the `From` header, this header is contrary to anonymization efforts. Again, the PGA HTTP proxy does not parse or remove this header but passes it through.

`TE` is a hop-by-hop header that indicates what extension transfer-codings a client is willing to accept in the response and whether or not it is willing to accept trailer fields in a chunked transfer-coding. Because the PGA Client HTTP proxy is not storing or recoding any data, it is passing through this header, even though passing-through of hop-by-hop headers is not intended by the HTTP specification.

`User-Agent` is an end-to-end header that contains information about the user agent originating the request. Similar to the `From` and `Referer` header, this header is contrary to anonymization efforts. Again, the PGA HTTP proxy does not parse or remove this header but passes it through.

`Proxy-Connection` is a non-standard header and the "correct" behavior when encountering this header is not defined. If a

[8]The word "referrer" is misspelled in the RFC as well as in most implementations.

```
Proxy-Connection: close
```

header is received, the PGA Client HTTP proxy closes the transport-level connection to the application after completing the HTTP response.

`Keep-Alive` is a non-standard header and the "correct" behavior when encountering this header is not defined. If a

```
Keep-Alive: Closed
```

header is received, the PGA Client HTTP proxy closes the transport-level connection to the application after completing the HTTP response.

Entity Headers

Entity headers define meta-information about the entity body or, if no body is present, about the resource identified by the request. HTTP/1.1 defines the following set of entity headers:

```
entity-header = Allow | Content-Encoding | Content-Language |
                Content-Length | Content-Location | Content-MD5 |
                Content-Range | Content-Type | Expires |
                Last-Modified
```

`Allow` is an end-to-end header that lists the set of methods supported by the resource identified by the Request-URI. The PGA Client HTTP proxy does not need to parse this header and must pass it through.

`Content-Encoding` is an end-to-end header that is used as a modifier to the `media-type`. When present, its value indicates what additional content codings have been applied to the entity-body (e.g. `gzip`), and thus what decoding mechanisms must be applied in order to obtain the media-type referenced by the `Content-Type` header field. The PGA Client HTTP proxy does not need to parse this header and must pass it through.

`Content-Language` is an end-to-end header that describes the natural language(s) of the intended audience for the enclosed entity. The PGA Client HTTP proxy does not need to parse this header and must pass it through.

`Content-Length` is an end-to-end header that indicates the size of the entity-body. The PGA Client HTTP proxy must parse this header to determine how much data can be forwarded in an efficient mode, without being parsed (this includes the whole message body) and when it must switch back to a mode where the data stream consists of HTTP requests that have to be parsed. In addition to being parsed, this header must be passed through unmodified.

`Content-Location` is an end-to-end header that is used to supply the resource location for the entity enclosed in the message when that entity is accessible from a location separate from the requested resource's URI. The PGA Client HTTP proxy does not need to parse this header and must pass it through.

`Content-MD5` is an end-to-end header that contains an MD5 digest of the entity-body for the purpose of providing an end-to-end message integrity check of the entity-body. The PGA Client HTTP proxy does not need to parse this header and must pass it through.

`Content-Range` is an end-to-end header that is sent with a partial entity-body to specify where in the full entity-body the partial body should be applied. The PGA Client HTTP proxy does not need to parse this header and must pass it through.

`Content-Type` is an end-to-end header that indicates the media type of the entity-body sent to the recipient. The PGA Client HTTP proxy does not need to parse this header and must pass it through.

`Expires` is an end-to-end header that gives the date/time after which the response is considered stale. The PGA Client HTTP proxy does not need to parse this header and must pass it through.

`Last-Modified` is an end-to-end header that indicates the date and time at which the origin server believes the variant was last modified. The PGA Client HTTP proxy does not need to parse this header and must pass it through.

4.3.2 Response Parsing

After extracting the address of the target system from an HTTP request, the PGA Client HTTP proxy translates the request into an internal API call of the PGA Client to establish an anonymous connection to the target system, translates the proxy request into a standard HTTP request, forwards the standard HTTP request and the request body to the target system. After receiving the request the target system will respond with a HTTP response message. These HTTP response messages will be transferred back to the PGA Server which forwards the messages anonymously back to the PGA Client until they are forwarded via the internal API to the PGA Client HTTP proxy, where the response messages have to be parsed again.

A response is a special HTTP message with the following syntax:

```
Response = Status-Line
           *((general-header |
              response-header|
              entity-header) CRLF)
           CRLF
           [ message-body ]
```

Status Line

The first line of a `Response` message is the `Status-Line`:

```
Status-Line = HTTP-Version SP Status-Code SP Reason-Phrase CRLF
```

It consists of the protocol version followed by a numeric status code and its associated textual phrase, with each element separated by `SP` characters. No `CR` or `LF` is allowed except in the final `CRLF` sequence.

`Status-Code` is a three-digit integer result code of the attempt to understand and satisfy the request.

`Reason-Phrase` is intended to give a short textual description of the `Status-Code`. The `Status-Code` is intended for use by automata and the `Reason-Phrase` is intended for the human user.

The PGA Client HTTP proxy transparently forwards the `Status-Line` to the application.

Response Headers

The response-headers allow the server to pass additional information about the response which cannot be placed in the `Status-Line`. HTTP/1.1 defines the following set of response headers:

```
response-header = Accept-Ranges | Age | ETag | Location |
                  Proxy-Authenticate | Retry-After | Server | Vary |
                  WWW-Authenticate
```

`Accept-Ranges` is an end-to-end header that allows the server to indicate its acceptance of range requests for a resource. The PGA Client HTTP proxy does not need to parse this header and must pass it through.

`Age` is an end-to-end header that conveys the sender's estimate of the amount of time since the response was generated at the origin server. The PGA Client HTTP proxy does not need to parse this header and must pass it through.

`ETag` is an end-to-end header that provides the current value of the entity tag for the requested variant. The PGA Client HTTP proxy does not need to parse this header and must pass it through.

`Location` is an end-to-end header that is used to redirect the recipient to a location other than the `Request-URI` for completion of the request or identification of a new resource. The PGA Client HTTP proxy does not need to parse this header and must pass it through.

`Proxy-Authenticate` is a hop-by-hop header that must be included as part of a 407 (Proxy Authentication Required) response. Because the PGA Client HTTP proxy, in its current form, never issues proxy authentication requests, it must ignore this header and remove it from the message.

`Retry-After` is an end-to-end header that can be used with a 503 (Service Unavailable) response to indicate how long the service is expected to be unavailable to the requesting client. The PGA Client HTTP proxy does not need to parse this header and must pass it through.

`Server` is an end-to-end header that contains information about the software used by the origin server to handle the request. The PGA Client HTTP proxy does not need to parse this header and must pass it through.

`Vary` is an end-to-end header that can be used to express the `request-header` fields the server used to select among multiple representations of a response subject to server-driven negotiation. The PGA Client HTTP proxy does not need to parse this header and must pass it through.

`WWW-Authenticate` is an end-to-end header that must be included in 401 (Unauthorized) response messages. The PGA Client HTTP proxy does not need to parse this header and must pass it through.

4.3.3 Message parsing

Header summary

The following table summarizes the actions the PGA Client HTTP proxy has to take for every header when parsing HTTP requests.

Table 4.1: PGA Client HTTP proxy actions with respect to HTTP message headers

header	ignore	parse	pass through	insert
`Accept`			X	
`Accept-Charset`			X	
`Accept-Encoding`			X	
`Accept-Language`			X	
`Accept-Ranges`			X	
`Age`			X	
`Allow`			X	
`Authorization`			X	
`Cache-Control`			X	
`Connection`		X		
`Content-Encoding`			X	

Continued on next page

Table 4.1 – continued from previous page

header	ignore	parse	pass through	insert
Content-Language			X	
Content-Length		X	X	
Content-Location			X	
Content-MD5			X	
Content-Range			X	
Content-Type			X	
Date			X	
ETag			X	
Expect			X	
Expires			X	
From			X	
Host			X	
If-Match			X	
If-Modified-Since			X	
If-None-Match			X	
If-Range			X	
If-Unmodified-Since			X	
Keep-Alive		X		
Last-Modified			X	
Location			X	
Max-Forwards	X			
Pragma			X	
Proxy-Authenticate	X			
Proxy-Authorization	X			
Proxy-Connection		X		
Range			X	
Referer			X	
Retry-After			X	
Server			X	
TE			X	

Continued on next page

Table 4.1 – continued from previous page

header	ignore	parse	pass through	insert
Trailer		X		
Transfer-Encoding		X		
Upgrade	X			
User-Agent			X	
Vary			X	
Via				X
Warning			X	
WWW-Authenticate			X	

All headers not enlisted in this table are passed through.

State machine

The PGA Client HTTP proxy must switch between the slow header parsing mode and the fast message body transfer mode. It does so by using the state machine shown in Figure 4.5 on page 54.

The PGA Client HTTP proxy starts and stays in header parsing mode until a complete header is parsed. A header is separated from the body with a CRLF (see HTTP message definition in section 4.3). When the header is completely parsed, the PGA Client HTTP proxy must determine if the message contains a body. This is only the case when a `Content-*` header is present. When the message contains a body, the PGA Client HTTP proxy must look for body size information. This can either be a `Content-Length` header or a `Transfer-Encoding: chunked` header. If the message contains body size information, the PGA Client HTTP proxy transfers the message body in a fast transfer mode (no parsing of any kind of data, just forwarding) and after that switches back to header parsing mode. If the message does not contain any body size information, the PGA Client HTTP proxy transfers the message body until the connection is closed and the state machine reaches it final state. (When the connection is closed, the final state is always reached. This was omitted from Figure 4.5 for better readability.)

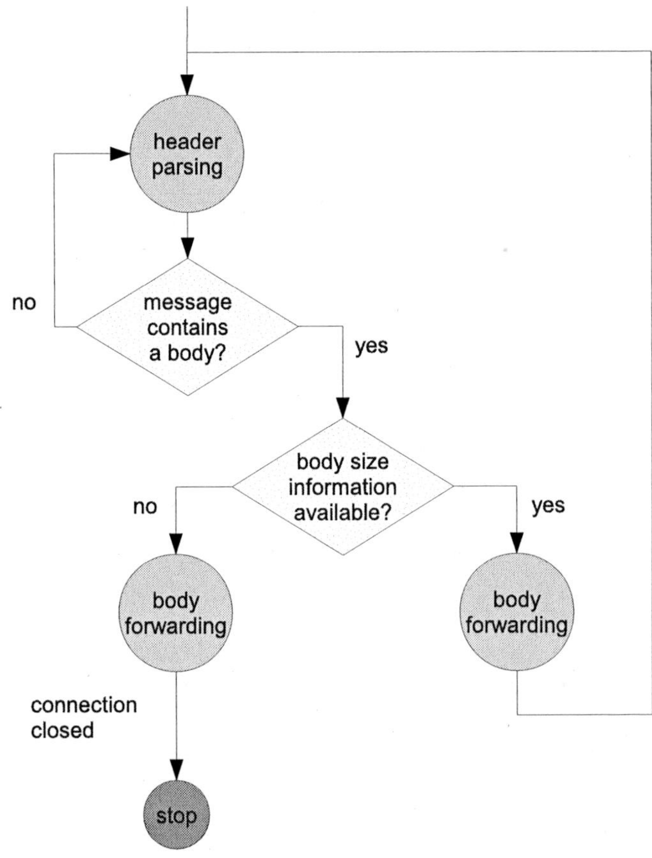

Figure 4.5: PGA Client HTTP proxy mode switching state machine

When the body size information is given with a `Content-Length` header, the state machine must forward exactly this number of bytes of body data to reach the beginning of the next header. When the message body is chunked, things are more complex. HTTP/1.1 defines the structure of a chunked body as follows:

```
Chunked-Body    = *chunk
                  last-chunk
                  trailer
                  CRLF
chunk           = chunk-size [ chunk-extension ] CRLF
                  chunk-data CRLF
chunk-size      = 1*HEX
last-chunk      = 1*("0") [ chunk-extension ] CRLF
chunk-extension= *( ";" chunk-ext-name [ "=" chunk-ext-val ] )
chunk-ext-name = token
chunk-ext-val   = token | quoted-string
chunk-data      = chunk-size(OCTET)
trailer         = *(entity-header CRLF)
```

The PGA Client HTTP proxy must parse and forward `chunk-sizes` and forward `chunk-data` until it encounters the `last-chunk` (a zero-length chunk). After that it must forward the trailer before switching back to header parsing mode.

4.3.4 Persistent connections

Already established anonymous connections between the PGA Client HTTP proxy and web servers should be re-used as often as possible to lower the computational overhead and the latency when requesting several entities from the same web server.

To be able to do so, the PGA Client HTTP proxy puts established connections into an internal register for every single proxy connection. Every register entry contains the server of the connection (host name and port), the ID used in the tunnel register (see section 4.6.3 on page 75) and the state of the upstream and downstream directions of the connection (see Figure 4.6). If an application issues a request to a server and the proxy register contains an entry to this server and both the upstream and downstream direction of the connection are still fully established,

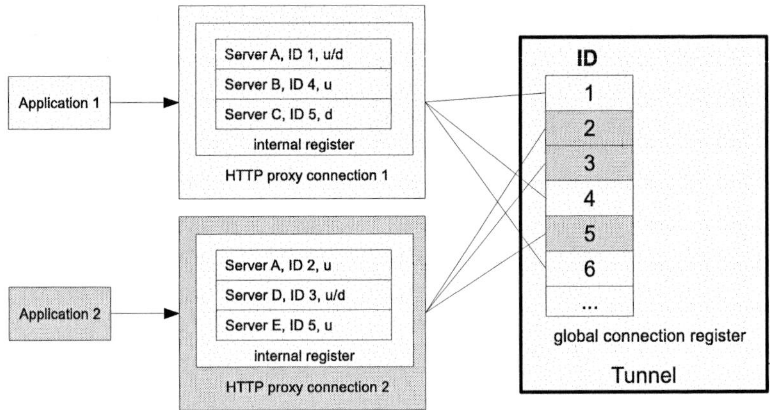

Figure 4.6: PGA Client HTTP proxy registers

the PGA Client HTTP proxy re-uses this connection. Otherwise it has to establish a new anonymous connection and add it to the internal register. Existing connections of other applications must not be re-used because this could leak sensible information from one application to another application.

If a web server closes a connection, the PGA Client HTTP proxy will not receive any more responses from this server via this connection (but the application could still send data to the web server via this connection). The connection has to be marked as "downstream closed" in the internal register.

If the application closes a connection, the PGA Client HTTP proxy will not receive any more requests from the application via this connection (but the web server could still send data to the application via this connection). The connection has to be marked as "upstream closed" in the internal register.

If an internal connection is both "downstream closed" and "upstream closed" it must be removed from the internal register.

4.4 Server

4.4.1 Core

The requirements for the PGA Server Core, defined by the author of this work, are as follows:

Application independence: The PGA Server Core must not be dependent on any application. It is sufficient to support tunneling of TCP/IP connections. Support for applications and protocols to be tunneled must be integrated into the PGA Client instead. This way the PGA Server Core can stay small, efficient, generic and support for additional applications and protocols can be integrated into PGA Clients without enforcing an upgrade on all PGA Server Cores.

Headless mode: The PGA Server Core must be able to run without a graphical user interface. This way it can be installed, run and maintained as a background process (called "service" or "daemon") on a server. Being able to run as a background process makes it much easier to automatically start, stop and restart the PGA Server Core via init scripts or manage it via service daemons like "at" [61] or "cron" [62].

Integrated firewall: Usually, the PGA Server Core should be operated in a demilitarized zone [38] where at least one firewall separates the internal network from the external network. Setting up a demilitarized zone is a non-trivial task and only supporting this setup would set the entry barrier for people wanting to offer an anonymization service unnecessary high. To support also small and simple installations of the PGA Server Core, it must be possible to install it in an internal network. To protect the internal network in this setup, the PGA Server Core must have an integrated firewall that must be able to prevent access from the external network to the internal network.

Anonymity group management: Anonymity groups are the essential part of anonymization in the PGA architecture. The PGA Server Core must be able to create these groups, add or remove users from anonymity groups (and generate and filter the associated dummy traffic) and also eventually delete anonymity groups when they are no longer needed.

User management: The PGA Server Core is transferring large volumes of data (especially when generating dummy traffic). This causes transmission costs that must be distributed among its users. Therefore the PGA Server Core must be able to manage its users and account and bill the traffic that every user generated or caused. On the other hand side it must also be possible to offer anonymization as a free service to anonymous users. Therefore the PGA Server Core must include an additional user management for anonymous users.

Misuse discouragement: The PGA Server Core and its operators act in an area of conflict. On one side it must deliver a trustworthy service to its users but on the other side it must prevent the misuse of exactly this service because it may lead to legal problems if illegal activities are originating from its infrastructure. To be able to really *prevent* misuses, the PGA Server Core must execute a very detailed analysis of all traffic before serving it. Because this detailed analysis is very computational intensive, it would slow down the anonymity service significantly. In addition to that, such measures would damage the reputation of anonymity providers because intensive monitoring is exactly the opposite of what users expect from a trustworthy anonymity provider.

A reasonable middle ground is to *discourage* misuse, i.e. not to prevent misuse but to be able to uncover it (after the fact) and react accordingly. Therefore the PGA Server Core must provide mechanisms to optionally log communication circumstances. This measure is relatively simple and does not slow down the service significantly.

Application independence Generic methods for establishing, managing and closing of anonymous TCP/IP connections have been integrated into the PGA tunnel protocol (see section 4.6 on page 67 for more details).

Headless mode Instead of a user interface, a management interface based on JMX (Java Management Extension) was integrated into the PGA Server core (see section 4.7 on page 101 for more details).

Integrated firewall The PGA Server Core keeps a list of internal networks and prevents access to these networks from all other networks. The management interface of the PGA Server Core provides several methods to manage the internal firewall:

`addInternalNetwork(cidrBlock:CIDRBlock)` adds a CIDR (Classless Inter-Domain Routing [47]) block to the list of internal networks

`setInternalNetwork(index:int, cidrBlock:CIDRBlock)` sets the CIDR block a specified index in the list of internal networks (this method is used to edit certain elements of the internal networks list).

`moveInternalNetworks(indices:int[], offset:int)` moves the specified indices of the internal networks list by a given offset (this method is used to reorder the internal networks list).

`removeInternalNetworks(indices:int[])` removes the specified indices from the list of internal networks.

`isLocalAccessBlocked()` returns `true`, if the internal firewall blocks access to all local networks (from the PGA Server Core's point of view), otherwise `false`

`setLocalAccessBlocked(localAccessBlocked:boolean)` determines, if the internal firewall blocks access to all local networks

Anonymity group management Today's common applications use many different protocols with many different bandwidth/delay properties (some examples are given in Figure 4.7 on page 60). There are protocols that need very little bandwidth, like SSH [3] and RSS [53]. SSH needs very short delays, otherwise working with interactive commands becomes very difficult. RSS on the other hand can handle longer delays without difficulty. A similar situation exists considering applications that need higher bandwidths, VoIP (Voice over Internet Protocol) needs to have very short delays to ensure the technical quality of the conversation (the ITU-T Recommendation G.114 [30] addresses delays for voice applications and declares that a delay of 150 milliseconds and shorter is acceptable and delays longer than 400 milliseconds are unacceptable), for a BitTorrent client, e.g. downloading the DVD image of a new Linux distribution, the delay between the downloaded packages is not as essential.

Because one requirement of the PGA Server Core is to be application independent, it should offer different anonymity groups for the different application/protocol classes explained above.

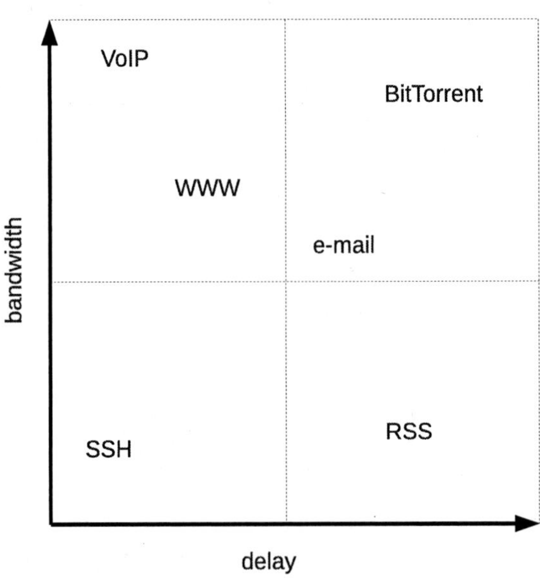

Figure 4.7: bandwidth/delay diagram of common protocols

The anonymity groups that are used in the PGA Server Core are defined as shown in the class diagram in Figure 4.8.

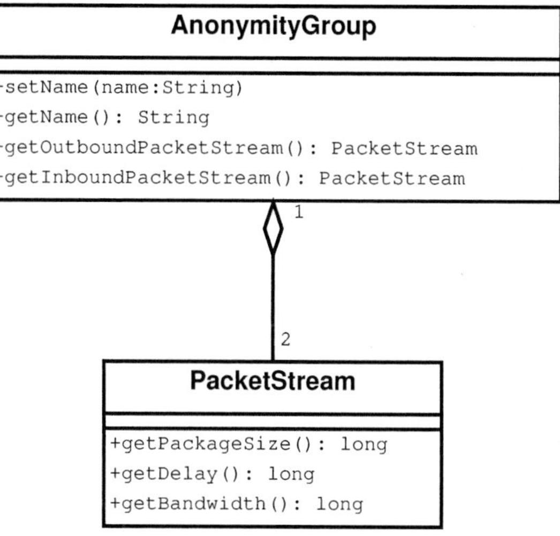

Figure 4.8: anonymity group class diagram

Every anonymity group has the following methods:

`setName(name:String)` sets the (descriptive and human-readable) name of this anonymity group.

`getName()` returns the name of this anonymity group

`getOutboundPacketStream()` returns the packet stream from the PGA Client to the PGA Server Core of this anonymity group

`getInboundPacketStream()` returns the packet stream from the PGA Server Core to the PGA Client of this anonymity group

Every package stream has the following methods:

`getPackageSize()` returns the size of the packages that have to be sent when using this package stream `getDelay()` returns the delay between sending packages when using this package stream

`getBandwidth()` returns the bandwidth of this package stream

Someone has to define the anonymity groups that can be used at a certain PGA Server Core. There were at least two different approaches to a solution:

User defined anonymity groups It is ultimately every single user who decides if, when and which anonymity group to join. Which anonymity group fits best with every user depends on many factors, including the bandwidth available to the user and the user's usage pattern (mainly used applications and protocols). From a user's point of view it would therefore seem obvious to let users create, manage and eventually delete anonymity groups on the PGA Server Core. In this case, a PGA Server operator will most probability want to restrict the number and the properties of the offered anonymity groups (maximum/minimum of package size and delay, some operators might even restrict the names of anonymity groups). Therefore a set of restrictions has to be managed.

Server defined anonymity groups Offering an anonymity group results in consuming of computational resources (calculating timeouts, generating random numbers, ...) and bandwidth (sending and filtering of dummy traffic). From an anonymity provider's point of view it would therefore seem obvious to define the available anonymity groups by a local and trusted system administrator and let the users choose between the offered anonymity groups.

It is even conceivable to use a mixture of both server and user defined anonymity groups.

User management

Account information When adding an account at a PGA Server Core, a user must provide some information:

- a pseudonym (mandatory)
- authentication credentials (mandatory)

- contact information (optional)
- a public key for encrypting communication, e.g. a GPG public key (optional)

The mandatory pseudonym must be a unique ID at the PGA Server Core so that all accounts (not necessarily all users) can be uniquely identified for all later purposes.

There are many authentication methods available today, all based on the authentication factors *knowledge* (e.g. a password), *ownership* (e.g. a security token), *inheritance* (e.g. a biometric identifier like a fingerprint) or a combination thereof. All authentication methods require to deposit some knowledge about the authentication factor (e.g. the password itself, the ID of a security token or a fingerprint template) at the authenticating instance, in this case the PGA Server Core.

The optional contact information can be used to e.g. send billing information or inform about changes in the anonymization service.

The optional public key can be used to ensure the confidentiality of the electronic communication with the user.

Billing Several billing models can be supported (e.g. flat rate, pay per used data volume, ...). Payment can be done either via non-anonymous methods (e.g. credit card, bank transfer, ...) or preferably with anonymous ecash payments [11, 12].

Account removal When a user removes an account at a PGA Server Core, the remaining balance of this account has to be credited (in addition to the actual account removal).

Anonymous users Because bandwidth and data transfer costs money it can become very expensive for a PGA Server operator to offer anonymization as a free service without imposing any limitation. Therefore it must be possible to define the following limits for anonymous users at the PGA Server Core:

maximum number of simultaneous anonymous users

maximum individual bandwidth of the tunnel between the PGA Client of an anonymous user and the PGA Server Core

maximum combined bandwidth as the maximum sum of all individual bandwidths

maximum data volume that can be transferred by anonymous users. This can be either of:

- a certain data volume
- a certain data volume in a certain interval
- no limit

Enforcing the *maximum combined bandwidth* can severely limit the service to anonymous users because it could lead to situations where anonymous users can no longer join an anonymity group or transfer *any* data.

Misuse discouragement The data retention function of the PGA Server Core records:

- time-stamp
- source IP
- destination host name
- resolved destination IP
- destination port
- success or failure of the connection attempt

There are several security mechanisms in the PGA architecture to make this function transparent for the users of the anonymity service and also to protect the anonymity service provider against itself:

User notification: For reasons of trust and transparency, users should be informed about the fact that the service they are using is recording connection attempts. Therefore, whenever the anonymity service provider switches the logging feature on or off, the PGA Server Core signals this circumstance immediately via the PGA tunnel protocol (see section 4.6 on page 67) to all users of the service as part of the dynamic server state (see section 4.2.1 on page 31) which is also exchanged when a PGA Client connects to a PGA Server Core and regularly requested by the PGA Client while connected to a PGA Server Core. The logging state of the PGA Server Core is displayed in the PGA Client user interface.

Encryption: In the PGA security model the anonymity provider is a trustworthy third party. Therefore it is not necessary to protect the logging information against the anonymity provider itself. But the anonymity service can be attacked by outsiders, i.e. the server where the logging information is stored can be stolen, confiscated or cracked. The recorded logging data is very sensitive personal data. Therefore it should always be stored on an encrypting file system. This protects the data in case of physical theft of the storage media. But if the anonymity service is compromised at runtime by cracking the system, the encrypted file system is usually in an "open" state, i.e. the system processes can read from and write data to it. This way an adversary could not only disclose all future communication circumstances but also all past communication circumstances stored in the logging data. To protect against this attack, the logging data itself must be encrypted before storing on the file system (each individual log file or, if using a database, each individual log entry). The logging data should be encrypted with a public key. An anonymity service provider could be bribed, blackmailed or forced to provide the decrypted logging information. Therefore, to make it impossible for the anonymity provider itself to decrypt the logging data, it is recommended to use an external public key for this task, e.g. the public key of a notary or a judge. This way the (already encrypted) logging data is also protected in case of software errors or unintentional configuration errors by staff members of the anonymity service.

Filtering: For a variety of reasons, some anonymity providers may not be interested in recording connection attempts. But those anonymity providers can still be forced by local authorities to record connections from a certain source address or to a certain destination address, e.g. to protocol access to websites illegal in the local jurisdiction. Therefore, the misuse discouragement system should be able to express filtering rules where the administrators of the anonymity service can specify which connection attempts are recorded and which are not.

Retention period: The recorded logs are automatically removed by the PGA Server Core after a configured retention period.

The definition of filters and a retention period are directed to the well established principle of data avoidance and data economy when dealing with personal data.

4.4.2 Remote Management

The requirements for the PGA Remote Management component are as follows:

Management protocol implementation: The PGA Remote Management must implement the PGA Remote Management protocol (see section 4.7) to manage the PGA Server Core.

Different user interfaces: To increase flexibility with respect to the form factor of possible administrative terminals ("normal" computers, smartphones, ...) and scenarios (on-site, local network, VPN, ...) the PGA Remote Management component must consist of different user interfaces (standalone application, web interface, ...) to the PGA Server Core.

Because the remaining design decisions regarding the PGA Remote Management component are very depended on the respective details of the PGA Remote Management protocol, they are described in section 4.7 (page 101).

4.5 Certificate Authority

Authentication and encryption of the tunnels between PGA Clients and PGA Server Cores is based on SSL [64]. To counter man-in-the-middle attacks, all PGA Clients and PGA Server Cores need to agree upon a set of trusted third parties that issue certificates for authentication and encryption.

While there are already many existing CAs, commercial and non-commercial, that could be used for this purpose, a simple CA for PGA has to be created, so that the PGA architecture becomes independent and self-contained.

The requirements for the PGA Certificate Authority are as follows:

CA Initialization: The PGA Certificate Authority must be able to initialize itself with a self-signed certificate.

Issuing of certificates: The PGA Certificate Authority must be able to issue certificates for PGA Server Cores based on certificate requests created by PGA Remote Management components. Requesting and signing certificates must adhere to established standards (certificate requests must be in PKCS#10 [41] and the issued certificates must adhere to X.509 [14]).

Graphical user interface: The PGA Certificate Authority must provide a graphical user interface for all its operations and configuration so that operators of the PGA Certificate Authority must not remember the syntax of commands but only have to deal with the semantics of requests and certificates.

The current design of the PGA CA is very simple and omits several building blocks of complete CA solutions like Certificate Revocation Lists [14] or CA certificate updates. These features can be added in future works.

4.6 Tunnel protocol

The protocol for information exchange through the SSL tunnel between a PGA Client and a PGA Server must support the following operations:

- User management (account opening, logging on and off, payments, account editing and account removal)
- Anonymity group management (joining and leaving an anonymity group, generating and filtering of dummy traffic)
- Connection management (open connections, transferring data, closing connections)
- Transfer of status information (e.g. uptime and load of the PGA Server Core)

4.6.1 Generic message format

Standard format

The most obvious way of exchanging all this different information is to put it into different messages. The next step is to decide the syntax and semantic of these messages. One can use a standardized message format or invent a proprietary one. The advantage of using a standardized message format (e.g. a stream of XML [8] entities or HTTP [17] messages with textual header and binary body) is that high quality generators and parsers already exist and the messages can be parsed by other programs following the same standard. The disadvantage is that the standardized message formats are more or less generic and use a lot of overhead regarding computational resources, memory consumption and transmission bandwidth. The advantage of using a proprietary message format is that it can be tailored exactly to the needs of the affected programs. The disadvantage is that proprietary generators and parsers have to be designed and implemented and as a result the messages can not be read by other programs.

With respect to the PGA architecture, messages are only exchanged between two programs, the PGA Client and the PGA Server Core. It is not necessary to parse the information by other programs or edit the messages by a normal user. In addition to that, the data exchange between a PGA Client and a PGA Server Core should be as fast and streamlined as possible to guarantee a high performance of the PGA Server Core. For all these reasons, a proprietary generic message format for the internal PGA tunnel protocol was designed.

Message framing

The most basic question that arises when designing a message protocol is how to specify where a message starts and where it ends. The SSL tunnel between a PGA Client and a PGA Server is based on TCP [9]. TCP is a stream protocol, i.e. it does not operate on data packages (collection or groups of bytes) but streams of single bytes. If messages are sent over TCP, their boundaries are not guaranteed. Messages can be merged, e.g. a sender sends two single messages "`The`" and "`rapist`", but the receiver receives the single message "`Therapist`". Single messages can be split, e.g. a sender sends "`Hello world`" in a single message but the receiver receives the two messages "`Hell`" and "`o world`". The only thing that TCP tries to guarantee is that the content and the order of bytes of a sent data stream is kept on the receiving side. The mechanism to ensure message boundaries when serializing/deserializing them over a data stream is called *message framing*.

The most common approaches used for message framing are:

Length prefixing: Every message is prefixed with the length of the message before sending both the prefix followed by the message. Because the length prefix itself is also composed of several bytes (to be able to specify large messages), it is also necessary to define the syntax and semantic of the length prefix. The receiving side must first read and parse the complete prefix so that the length of the following message becomes known. Then the complete message has to be read before the next prefix is read and parsed. A denial-of-service attack at the receiver's side is possible by specifying a very large message size in the prefix. This can be countered by making the length of the prefix reasonably small or by specifying a maximum message size.

Delimiters: A chosen combination of bytes is selected as the message boundaries, the delimiters. The sender of a message must escape every occurrence of delimiters in the message itself with an escaping function that also has to be defined, e.g. by prefixing the delimiters with *another* chosen combination of bytes or by doubling all occurrences of delimiters. The receiving side must read the stream of bytes until a delimiter is found. After that the unescaping function (the inverse of the escaping function) must be applied to all received data (excluding the delimiter itself) to get the original message. A denial-of-service attack at the receiver's side is possible by not sending any delimiter. This attack can only be countered by specifying a maximum message size.

Because, in contrast to delimiters, length prefixing does not need an escaping and unescaping function and prevention of denial-of-service attacks is easier, it is used in the PGA Tunnel Protocol to frame messages. To be able to transmit reasonably large data packages and still defend against denial-of-service attacks, the prefix length is set to a length of two bytes (in the standard, big-endian [13] network byte order), so that the maximum message length of the PGA Tunnel Protocol is $2^{(2 \cdot 8)} = 2^{16} = 65535$ bytes.

4.6.2 Message syntax and semantic

While message framing alone ensures message boundaries, it does not define the internal structure of the transmitted messages. Therefore, the syntax and the semantic of all PGA Tunnel Protocol messages has to be defined.

The basic internal message structure is similar to *length prefixing* above, but this time the prefix does not denote the *length* of the message but the *type* of its *value*. Therefore it is called *type prefixing*. Because the number of different message types in the PGA Tunnel Protocol is quite manageable, the length of the type prefix is set to only one single byte, so that a maximum of $2^8 = 255$ different message types can be specified.

The following message types are already defined in the PGA Tunnel Protocol:

`LOCALE` This message is sent from the PGA Client to the PGA Server Core and contains information about the user's locale (language and region). This information is needed for supporting localized status information and error messages so that users actually understand the human-readable messages coming from the PGA Server Core. The internal structure of this message is a locale definition with the following syntax:

```
locale   = language "_" region
language = 1*ALPHA
region   = 1*ALPHA
```

Examples:

- Swiss German: `de_CH`
- American English: `en_US`

`STATIC_STATE` This message is sent only once from the PGA Server Core to the PGA Client directly after establishing the tunnel between them and contains the static status information of the PGA Server Core (for details of the static server status please see the definition of the class `StaticServerState()` in section 4.2.1 on page 31). The internal format of this message is an XML structure holding a textual representation of the static server status (see section 6.2 on page 141).

`STATE_REQUEST` This message is sent regularly from the PGA Client to the PGA Server Core to request an update on the dynamic state (see below for details) of the PGA Server Core. This message consists only of its type prefix.

`DYNAMIC_STATE` Whenever a PGA Server Core receives a `STATE_REQUEST` message (see above) from a PGA Client, it is supposed to respond with a `DYNAMIC_STATE` message (for details of the dynamic server status please see the definition of the class `DynamicServerState()` in section 4.2.1 on page 31). The PGA Server Core does not actively send this message but only when requested, because every PGA Client can have different features or settings with respect to if and how often the dynamic server state is displayed to its users. The internal format of this message is an XML structure holding a textual representation of the dynamic server status (see section 6.2 on page 141).

`OPEN` This message is part of the PGA connection handling (see section 4.6.3 on page 76) and is sent from a PGA Client to a PGA Server Core whenever a new anonymous connection must be established. It has the following syntax:

```
OPEN            = client-side-ID
                  address-length
                  address
                  payload
client-side-ID = <2OCTET in network byte order>
address-length = <2OCTET in network byte order>
address         = hostname ":" portnumber
hostname        = <any OCTET except ":">
portnumber      = 1*DIGIT
payload         = *OCTET
```

When receiving an `OPEN` message, a PGA Server Core extracts the client side connection ID and the target address, tries to establish a TCP connection to the specified target address. If the connection could be successfully established, the PGA Server Core sends the payload to the target address, if the connection could *not* be successfully established, the PGA Server Core silently discards the payload.

`OPEN_SUCCEEDED` This message is part of the PGA connection handling (see section 4.6.3 on page 76) and is sent from the PGA Server Core to the PGA Client when a connection to a target address specified in an `OPEN` message (see above) could be successfully established. It has the following syntax:

```
OPEN_SUCCEEDED = client-side-ID
                 server-side-ID
client-side-ID = <2OCTET in network byte order>
server-side-ID = <2OCTET in network byte order>
```

`OPEN_FAILED` This message is part of the PGA connection handling (see section 4.6.3 on page 76) and is sent from the PGA Server Core to the PGA Client when a connection to a target address specified in an `OPEN` message (see above) could *not* be successfully established. It has the following syntax:

```
OPEN_FAILED    = client-side-ID
                 error-message
client-side-ID = <2OCTET in network byte order>
error-message  = *OCTET
```

`DATA` This message is part of the PGA message tunneling protocol (see section 4.6.3 on page 77) and is sent from either the PGA Server Core or the PGA Client to transparently transfer data that was read from the application or server at the respective target connection. It has the following syntax:

```
DATA          = connection-ID
                payload
connection-ID = <2OCTET in network byte order>
payload       = *OCTET
```

`XOFF` This message is part of the PGA flow control mechanism (see section 4.6.4 on page 88) and is used to stop the peer side from reading data from the target connection. It has the following syntax:

```
XOFF          = connection-ID
connection-ID = <2OCTET in network byte order>
```

`XON` This message is part of the PGA flow control mechanism (see section 4.6.4 on page 88) and is used to resume reading data from the target connection at the peer side. It has the following syntax:

```
XON           = connection-ID
connection-ID = <2OCTET in network byte order>
```

`JOIN` This message is sent from the PGA Client to the PGA Server Core to join a specified anonymity group. It has the following syntax:

```
JOIN            = anonymity-group
anonymity-group = 1*OCTET
```

`JOIN_SUCCEEDED` When a PGA Client could successfully join an anonymity group, the respective PGA Server Core responses with this message to indicate the success of the join operation. This message consists only of its type prefix.

`JOIN_FAILED` When a PGA Client could *not* successfully join an anonymity group, the respective PGA Server Core responses with this message to indicate the failure of the join operation and the reason of the failure. It has the following syntax:

```
JOIN_FAILED   = error-message
error-message = 1*OCTET
```

`LEAVE` This message is sent from the PGA Client to the PGA Server Core to leave the currently joined anonymity group. This message consists only of its type prefix.

`SHUTDOWN` This message is part of the PGA connection handling (see section 4.6.3 on page 77) and is sent from either the PGA Client or the PGA Server Core to shut down one direction of an anonymous connection. It has the following syntax:

```
SHUTDOWN      = connection-ID
connection-ID = <2OCTET in network byte order>
```

`ERROR` This message is part of the PGA connection handling (see section 4.6.3 on page 77) and is sent from either the PGA Client or the PGA Server Core to shut down an anonymous connection in case of a local input/output error. It has the following syntax:

```
ERROR         = connection-ID
connection-ID = <2OCTET in network byte order>
```

4.6.3 Message tunneling

Anonymous connections in the PGA architecture are data streams that originate mostly from applications and terminate at a web server. In between there is the anonymizing architecture, the PGA Client and the PGA Server Core (see Figure 4.9.

The applications and servers do not know about the PGA architecture at all and have their communication handled by normal TCP streams. Between the PGA

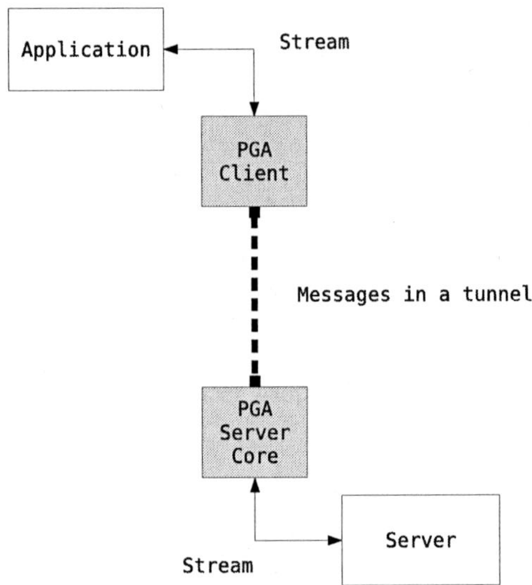

Figure 4.9: Messages in PGA tunnel

Client and the PGA Server Core there is one single data stream wherein the distinguished messages defined above are exchanged. This architecture must solve the following two challenges:

- (De)multiplexing streams with messages
- Flow control

(De)multiplexing streams with messages

Connection register

Figure 4.9 is an oversimplification. In normal situations there are several applications talking to the PGA Client at the same time, maybe some of those applications having several connections open simultaneously. At the tunnel side there is normally quite a number of PGA Clients talking to one single PGA Server Core which itself is communicating with lots of servers.

This all leads to the situation where there are several streams sharing one resource: the tunnel between the PGA Client and the PGA Server Core. Because the only way to communicate through the tunnel is sending some messages, the messages of one stream have to be "tagged" somehow, so that they can be correlated. To solve this problem, the PGA architecture uses a separate *connection register* for every single tunnel.

There are several ways to implement such a connection register, e.g. an array or a hash table. Accessing elements of an array is much faster than retrieving values out of a hash table. Therefore an array is used in the PGA architecture. One disadvantage of arrays is that they can not be stored as densely as a hash table. If both connection indices `0` and `60.000` are used, the register array needs to have allocated memory for at least 60.000 entries. A hash table would only need two entries in this case.

This characteristic of arrays opens the door for a denial-of-service attack: When the PGA Client decides on the connection indices it could request a connection with a very high index and the PGA Server Core must allocate a large array to store the connection reference. If a compromised PGA Client does this with a large number of tunnels, the PGA Server Core must allocate a significant amount of memory or even runs out of memory. Because of this threat the connection indices are not handled by (untrusted) PGA Clients but the PGA Server Core itself.

Opening connections

Every time an application requests a new connection, the PGA Client generates a temporary but unique ID for this connection and stores the pair of (ID, connection) somewhere. The ID can be generated randomly or simply be an increasing sequence.

In addition to that, the PGA Client tries to read as much data from the application as possible. The temporary ID, the requested target address and the initial data are the components of the first message of a new connection: the `OPEN` message sent by the PGA Client to the PGA Server Core (see definition of the `OPEN` message on page 71).

For example, a web browser sends the following request to the PGA Client Web Connector:

```
GET http://www.example.org:8080/example.html HTTP/1.1
```

The PGA Client Web Connector parses the HTTP request and extracts the target address `www.example.org:8080`. Then it translates the HTTP proxy request into a normal HTTP request:

```
GET /example.html HTTP/1.1
Host: www.example.org:8080
```

The PGA Client generates the unique index `4711`, stores the pair of `4711` and this connection somewhere and creates the following `OPEN` message (`|` denotes the message element boundaries):

```
4711 | 20 | www.example.org:8080 | GET /example.html HTTP/1.1\r\n
Host: www.example.org:8080
```

When the PGA Server Core receives an `OPEN` message it first extracts and stores the unique ID. Then it parses the address length as an integer value (20 in the example above). The length value is used to read in the address part. Then it tries to connect to the specified target address. If the connection to the target address failed, the PGA Server Core sends an `OPEN_FAILED` message (see definition on page 71) to the PGA Client. The `OPEN_FAILED` message must contain the stored unique ID from the associated `OPEN` message so that the PGA Client can correlate both messages. In addition to that it may contain a detailed error message explaining why the connection failed (e.g. the target name could not be resolved or the connection was refused by the target).

For example:

```
4711 | Unable to connect to remote host: Connection refused
```

If the connection to the target address succeeds, the PGA Server Core first searches for a free index in its connection register. If there is no free index available it enlarges the array by five entries and uses the next free entry.

Now the PGA Server Core sends an `OPEN_SUCCEEDED` message (see definition on page 71) to the PGA Client. As with the `OPEN_FAILED` message, the `OPEN_SUCCEEDED` message must also contain the unique ID from the associated `OPEN` message so that the PGA Client can correlate both messages. In addition to that it must contain the index of this new connection in the PGA Server connection register.

For example, when the next free entry in the tunnel register at the PGA Server Core was `815`, the `OPEN_SUCCEEDED` message would look like this:

```
4711 | 815
```

After notifying the PGA Client with the `OPEN_SUCCEEDED` message that the new connection was successfully established, the PGA Server Core sends the initial data (payload) to the target system. Now it becomes obvious that having the initial data in the `OPEN` message reduces the latency of the PGA architecture. Otherwise the PGA Client would have to wait for the `OPEN_SUCCEEDED` message to arrive from the PGA Server Core before tunneling the first real connection data via `DATA` messages.

Data exchange

After establishing an anonymous connection as described above, application data can be transferred. This is done via `DATA` messages. These messages are always sent when either the PGA Client has read some data from the application or the PGA Server Core from the target system. Because there can be `DATA` packages from many different connections flowing through one tunnel between a PGA Client and a PGA Server Core, the `DATA` messages must be tagged with the connection ID.

When either the PGA Client or the PGA Server Core receives a `DATA` message it must first extract the connection ID and then retrieve a reference to the corresponding connection from its connection register. Then it must forward the user data to the connection endpoint (the application on PGA Client side or the target system on PGA Server Core side).

Closing connections

Shutting down TCP/IP connections is more difficult than opening them. A TCP/IP connection consists of two endpoints and two directions (see Figure 4.10). The upstream and downstream directions can be closed asymmetrically. That means that even if one direction of a connection is closed, data can still be transferred into the other direction.

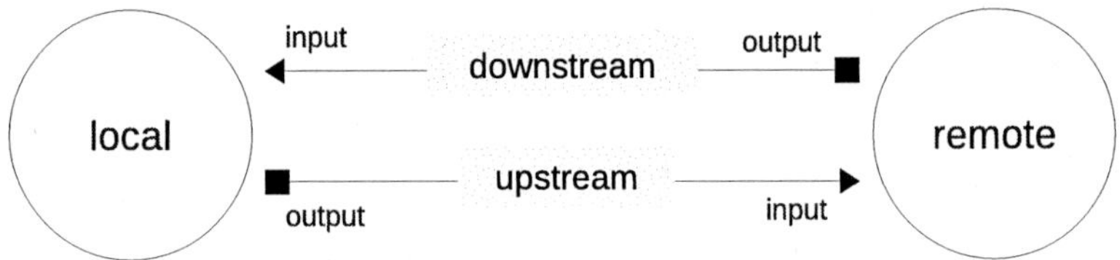

Figure 4.10: Endpoints and directions in a TCP/IP connection

Because anonymous connections of the PGA architecture are established over three independent TCP/IP connections (application ↔ PGA Client ↔ PGA Server Core ↔ target), all TCP shutdown events have to be passed as messages through the PGA architecture.

Regular shutdown

Because the following description applies to "Application ↔ PGA Client" as well as "PGA Server Core ↔ Target" connections, the generic terms "PGA" for both PGA Client and PGA Server Core and "endpoint" for the application and the target system is used here.

If PGA receives a TCP FIN[9] package from the endpoint it must mark the connection as "write only" and must send a `SHUTDOWN` message through the tunnel. This message just contains the associated connection ID. (It is still possible to forward data to the endpoint. Therefore PGA must not close the connection completely yet.) When PGA receives a `SHUTDOWN` message it must mark the connection as "read only" and send a TCP FIN packet to the endpoint. When a connection is marked both as "write only" and "read only" it must be closed and removed from the corresponding index in the connection register.

[9]a TCP FIN (finish) package signals that there will be no more data packages coming from the sender

Exceptional shutdown

Sometimes it may happen that PGA does not receive a TCP FIN or RST[10] package from an endpoint, e.g. when the endpoint's operation system crashed or the network between PGA and the endpoint was physically disconnected. PGA will notice this problem only when trying to write to the endpoint (e.g. transfer some user data or deliver an error message).

There is an even more difficult situation that must be handled by the PGA communication infrastructure: Both endpoints (the application at the PGA Client side and the target system at the PGA Server Core side) crash simultaneously while no `DATA` packages are on their way. Because there are no pending write operations the PGA communication infrastructure would not detect the crashes and end up with idle connections that would never be cleaned up. Therefore the TCP "alive" feature is used: When a connection was idle for a long time (the exact time span depends on the operating system) a TCP package without any payload is send and must be acknowledged by the receiver. If the receiver doesn't respond to the "alive" package the sender must assume that the receiver has crashed or disconnected.

If a network error occurs at the PGA Client side it must send an `ERROR` message to the PGA Server Core and remove the connection from the corresponding index in the connection register. When the PGA Server Core receives an `ERROR` message it must close the connection and remove the connection from the corresponding index in the connection register.

The complete state machine for PGA Client target connections is shown in Figure 4.11.

Network errors at the PGA Server Core side must be handled with more care. The example shown in Figure 4.12 demonstrates the problem:

- D_{x1} is the first `DATA` package of connection x
- OC_y is the `OPEN` message of connection y
- D_{x2} is the second `DATA` package of connection x

If writing D_{x1} generates a network error and the error handling would be exactly as on the PGA Client side, the following problem could arise:

1. the connection register index of connection x is freed

[10] a TCP RST (reset) package closes a connection

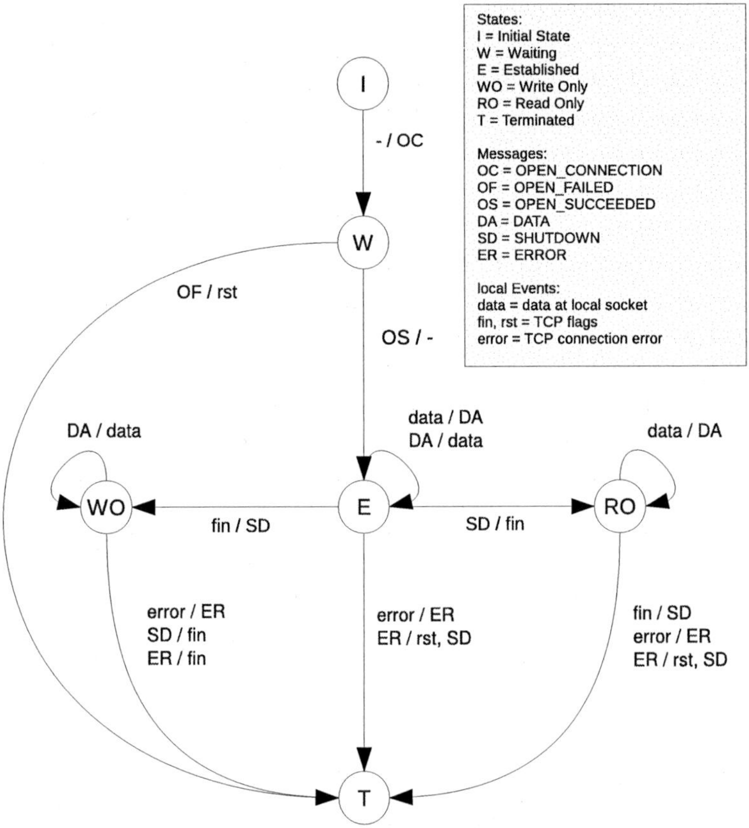

States:
I = Initial State
W = Waiting
E = Established
WO = Write Only
RO = Read Only
T = Terminated
Messages:
OC = OPEN_CONNECTION
OF = OPEN_FAILED
OS = OPEN_SUCCEEDED
DA = DATA
SD = SHUTDOWN
ER = ERROR
local Events:
data = data at local socket
fin, rst = TCP flags
error = TCP connection error
I
- / OC
W
OF / rst
OS / -
DA / data
data / DA
DA / data
data / DA
WO
E
RO
fin / SD
SD / fin
error / ER
SD / fin
ER / fin
error / ER
ER / rst, SD
fin / SD
error / ER
ER / rst, SD
T

Figure 4.11: State machine for PGA Client target connections

PGA Server Core
D_{x1}
OC_y
D_{x2}

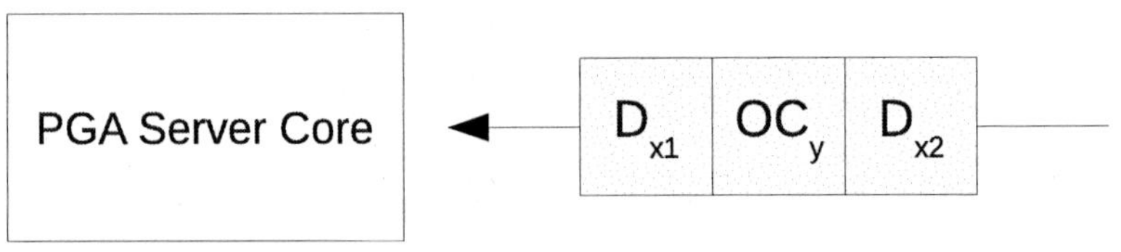

Figure 4.12: Example of incoming messages at the PGA Server Core

2. the `OPEN` message is processed and the register index of connection x is reused

3. D_{x2} is written to the endpoint of connection y and thereby leaking information to a wrong endpoint. This is not only a severe security problem but may also cause application protocol errors.

To prevent this scenario from happening, additional states, similar to the CLOSE-WAIT and FIN-WAIT states of the TCP finite state machine [31] is necessary. Because the PGA tunneling protocol sits on top of TCP, the solution can be much simpler than the TCP finite state machine. Therefore, an additional "pending" state for PGA Server Core target connections is introduced wherein it has to wait for the remaining packages of the connection to arrive before termination and reusing the target register index becomes possible:

Whenever a network error occurs at the PGA Server Core side it must send an `ERROR` message to the PGA Client. When there may still be `DATA` packages coming (the PGA Server Core connection is fully established or in state "write only") the connection must move to the "pending" state. If the PGA Client receives an `ERROR` message it must acknowledge this message with a `SHUTDOWN` message (if not already sent in the meantime). The PGA server connection must only leave the "pending" state when receiving a `SHUTDOWN` message or (if a network error occurs simultaneously on both PGA Client and PGA Server Core side) an `ERROR` message.

The complete state machine for PGA Server Core target connections is shown in Figure 4.13.

Model Checking

It is fundamentally impossible to construct a general proof procedure for arbitrary programs (the unsolvability of the halting problem was proven by Alan Turing in 1936 [63]). However, the correctness of a distributed software system can be "mechanically" verified with simple tool-based verification techniques, e.g. a logic model checker.

Quoting the preface of SPIN [28]:

> A logic model checker is designed to use efficient procedures for characterizing all possible executions, rather than a small subset, as one might see in trial executions. Since it can explore all behaviors, the model checker can apply a range of sanity checks to the design model, and it

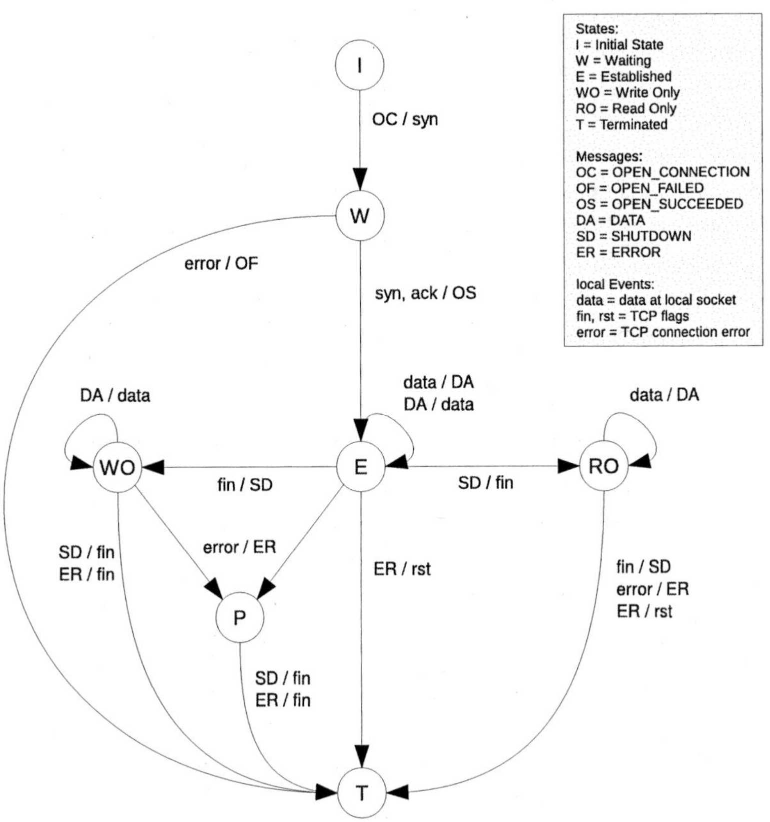

Figure 4.13: State machine for PGA Server Core target connections

> can successfully identify non-executable code, or potentially deadlocking concurrent situations. It can even check for compliance with complex user-defined correctness criteria. Model checkers are unequally in their ability to locate subtle bugs in system designs, providing far greater control than the more traditional methods based on human inspection, testing or random simulation.

The Spin model checker (`http://spinroot.com`[11]) was used to verify the design of the concurrent connection state machines used for PGA Client and PGA Server Core. So that Spin can simulate and verify the state machine models they must be build in `ProMeLa` (*Pro*cess *Me*ta-*La*nguage), an abstract system description language. The `ProMeLa` source code is shown in appendix A.1.

Simulation

With the following command:

```
spin -c <promela_file>
```

the system modeled within the specified `ProMeLa` file is simulated. One possible run is executed and is printed on screen. A simulation run may vary each time. A possible run could look like this:

```
proc 0 = PGA_Client
proc 1 = PGA_Server
q\p   0   1
  1   client_to_server!OPEN
  1   .   client_to_server?OPEN
  2   .   server_to_client!OPEN\_SUCCEEDED
  2   server_to_client?OPEN\_SUCCEEDED
  2   .   server_to_client!DATA
  2   .   server_to_client!DATA
  2   server_to_client?DATA
  2   .   server_to_client!DATA
  1   client_to_server!DATA
  2   .   server_to_client!DATA
```

[11]last visited: January 2012

```
  2   .   server_to_client!DATA
  1   client_to_server!DATA
  2   .   server_to_client!DATA
  2   .   server_to_client!DATA
  1   .   client_to_server?DATA
  1   client_to_server!DATA
  1   client_to_server!SHUTDOWN
  1   client_to_server!ERROR
      PGA Client reached TERMINAL state
  2   .   server_to_client!ERROR
  1   .   client_to_server?DATA
  1   .   client_to_server?DATA
  1   .   client_to_server?SHUTDOWN
          PGA Server reached TERMINAL state
-------------
final state:
-------------
2 processes created
```

Verification

To verify a system model two steps need to be taken. The first step tells SPIN to generate C code from the given system model defined within the ProMeLa file:

```
spin -a <promela_file>
```

The second step then compiles the program:

```
gcc -o pan pan.c
```

This creates an executable file called pan. When pan is executed the program checks if any errors can be found. Generally every possible transition and state combinations is checked for variable inconsistencies. A successful system would generate 0 errors and the output would look like this:

```
(Spin Version 4.2.9 -- 8 February 2007)
        + Partial Order Reduction
```

```
Full statespace search for:
        never claim             - (none specified)
        assertion violations    +
        acceptance   cycles     - (not selected)
        invalid end states      +

State-vector 44 byte, depth reached 150, errors: 0
    2953 states, stored
    4084 states, matched
    7037 transitions (= stored+matched)
       0 atomic steps
hash conflicts: 7 (resolved)

2.724   memory usage (Mbyte)

unreached in proctype PGA_Client
        (0 of 43 states)
unreached in proctype PGA_Server_Core
        (0 of 49 states)
```

The verification of the PGA connection state machines did not find any errors, i.e. deadlocks, unreachable states or time outs.

4.6.4 Flow control

End-to-End flow control

Motivation

Communication over unreliable media is a difficult task. Because the PGA tunnel protocol is built on top of TCP the most difficult problems (package loss, duplication, reordering, ...) are already solved by TCP's own mechanisms.

One of the problems that TCP solves in a very sophisticated way is flow control. Flow control is the process of adjusting the flow of data from a sender to a receiver to ensure that the receiver can handle all of the incoming data. This is particularly important where senders and receivers are unmatched in capacity and processing power, especially when the sender is capable of sending data much faster than the receiver can handle it. TCP uses a *sliding window* protocol (see section 3.4 of [60]) to solve the flow control problem.

The PGA tunneling protocol is build on top of TCP. Therefore, the data channel from the application to the server in figure 4.9 (on page 74) is reliable. But a new problem arises because the PGA tunnel protocol works over a chain of the following three independent TCP links:

- Application ↔ PGA Client
- PGA Client ↔ PGA Server Core
- PGA Server Core ↔ Server

In this situation all reliability features of TCP still apply for the connection from the application to the server except flow control. This is very problematic in certain situations, like in the following example:

The connection from the application to the PGA Client and the connection from the PGA Client to the PGA Server Core are high bandwidth links (see figure 4.14, higher bandwidth is illustrated by thicker lines). The connection between the PGA Server Core and the server is a low bandwidth connection (illustrated by a thinner line). If the application sends `DATA` packages to the server with all its available bandwidth it would not take very long and the PGA Server Core would not be able to deliver the packages to the server. The packages must be buffered at the PGA Server Core until the server can receive more data. Without any additional mechanisms, the application could fill up the buffer space of the PGA Server Core and in this way bringing down the PGA service completely. This situation motivates an additional layer of flow control mechanism in the PGA tunneling protocol.

Figure 4.14: Flow control problem with PGA tunneling protocol

Evaluation

There are many known flow control mechanisms. In this section some common mechanisms are introduced and evaluated regarding their applicability for the PGA tunneling protocol.

For all mechanisms we assume that the tunneling protocol sits on top of a reliable TCP connection (packages are not lost).

There is a common attack against availability at the PGA Server Core that we consider for every evaluated flow control mechanism: The adversary tries to fill up as much buffer space at the PGA Server Core as possible.

Request/Reply

Request/reply flow control requires each data packet to be acknowledged by the remote host before the next packet is sent. Sometimes referred to as ping-pong behavior, request/reply is simple to understand and implement.

The request/reply flow control mechanism has a major disadvantage: it is not very efficient. At any given point in time there can be only one data package on its way through the tunnel. This wastes a lot of network capacity (the *bandwidth· delay* product of the tunnel).

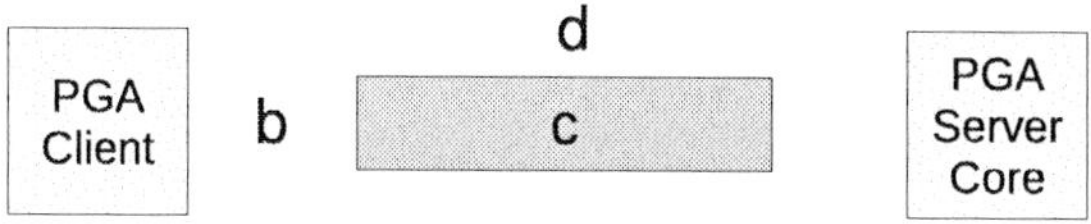

Figure 4.15: Tunnel capacity

In figure 4.15 b is the bandwidth of the tunnel, d is the delay of the connection, and $c = b \cdot d$ is the network capacity of the tunnel.

If the request/reply flow control mechanism is used in the PGA tunneling protocol, a new `REQUEST` message would have to be introduced. This message would have to be send by the PGA components when a write operation was completed and no buffered data is left. If a PGA component receives a `DATA` package despite no `REQUEST` message was sent beforehand, it would be able to assume that the PGA peer is compromised and may terminate the tunnel connection.

To fill up as much buffer space at the PGA Server as possible, the following attack can be executed: An adversary starts two software components, a sender and a receiver. The sender uses the PGA infrastructure to connect to the receiver. After establishing the connection the receiver stops reading data from the PGA Server, thereby forcing the PGA Server to buffer data. The sender may now send one maximum size `DATA` package. The maximum size of `DATA` packages in the current PGA tunnel protocol is $2^{16} - 4 = 65532$ byte. This is a comparatively small value and poses no real threat to the PGA Server Core availability.

XON/XOFF

In this simple flow control mechanism, the receiver sends an `XOFF` message to the sender when its buffer is full. The sender then stops sending data. When the receiver is ready to receive more data, it sends an `XON` signal. Therefore the `XON/XOFF` mechanism very efficiently uses the available bandwidth. Despite being a flow control mechanism it is no congestion avoidance mechanism. `XON/XOFF` only becomes effective when a congestion already happened.

This leads to a typical stop-and-go behavior of the traffic when congestion appears as shown in figure 4.16.

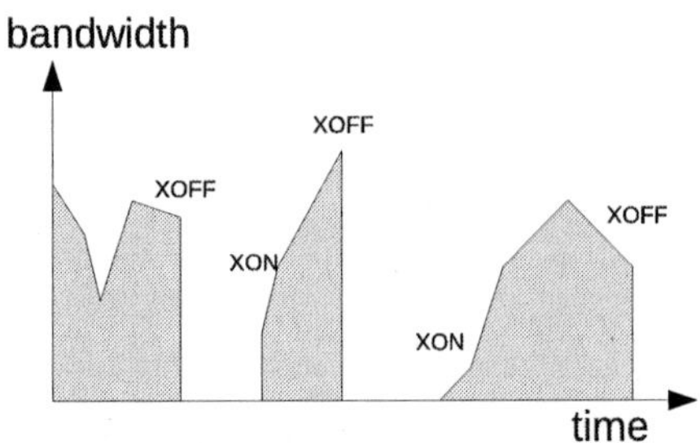

Figure 4.16: Traffic pattern in saturated network using `XON/XOFF`

The messages in the PGA tunneling protocol do not share a common header where the flow control messages could be integrated into. Therefore two new message types for the messages `XON` and `XOFF` have to be introduced.

If the PGA Server Core is unable to write a `DATA` package completely to a server it must buffer the remaining data. If this buffer reaches a certain size limit the PGA Server Core must send an `XOFF` message to the PGA Client as a congestion indication. When receiving an `XOFF` message, the PGA Client should stop reading new data from its regarding application. When the PGA Server Core is later able to write data from the buffer to the server so that the buffer size falls below the size limit it must send an `XON` message to the PGA Client. When receiving an `XON` message the PGA Client must start again reading new data from its local application. Because the underlying TCP already has write buffers it is perfectly valid to set the normal buffer size limit to zero. That means, whenever an incomplete write operation occurs at a PGA component, an `XOFF` message must be sent.

An adversary could impose both sender and receiver and stop reading data at the receiver side. Then the attacker's PGA Client could ignore the `XOFF` message (send by the PGA Server Core) and continue sending data, this way filling up the PGA Server Core buffer space. A countermeasure to this attack is possible: After sending the `XOFF` message the PGA Server may accept new `DATA` packages only for a short period of time. This period must not be much longer longer as the average RTT (round-trip-time) for the tunnel. There are ways to measure the tunnel RTT if the PGA Client is not compromised. Because compromised PGA Clients may even manipulate RTT measurement, the time period must be a constant value that is somewhat larger than typical Internet RTT's. If, after sending `XOFF` and accepting new `DATA` packages for the RTT period, the PGA Server still receives new `DATA` packages it may assume that the PGA Client is compromised and terminate the tunnel.

Any PGA Client (normal or attacking) with a very high bandwidth connection to the PGA Server Core could fill up the available buffer space during the `XOFF` time out period mentioned above. Therefore a second buffer size limit has to be specified. When reaching this "emergency" limit the PGA Server must stop reading from the tunnel completely until the buffer size falls again under this limit. This would stop all connections served by the tunnel instead of only the one with a congested peer. This again would be very irritating for non-attacking PGA Client users.

All mechanisms described above naturally also apply for the opposite direction (PGA Client $\rightarrow$ PGA Server Core).

The `XON`/`XOFF` flow control mechanism is very efficient because there are no computational or bandwidth resources used at all when there is no congestion happening. When looking at typical bandwidth distributions for PGA tunnels (see figure 4.17), it is clear that congestion is rather the exception than the norm in PGA tunnels.

The application and the PGA Client are almost always running on the same machine, therefore using a local link with a very high bandwidth. In contrast to that

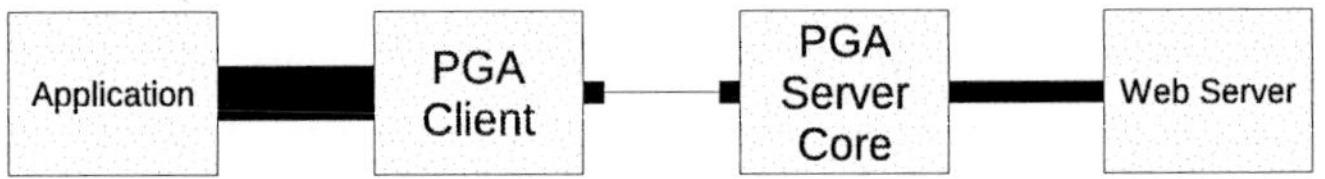

Figure 4.17: Typical bandwidth distribution for PGA tunnels

the tunnel between PGA Client and PGA Server Core is relatively low bandwidth because computational intensive encryption is used and the Internet link of one PGA Server Core is simultaneously shared between all its connected PGA Clients. The bandwidth is especially low if the PGA Client is a member of a low-bandwidth anonymity group. The connection between a PGA Server and a usual web server is mostly a normal bandwidth connection.

In summary, the `XON/XOFF` flow control mechanism is very efficient but in worst case scenarios congestion control and attack resistance is neither elegant nor simple.

Sliding window

A simplified version of the TCP sliding window flow control mechanism could be used for the PGA tunneling protocol. In contrast to the `XON/XOFF` protocol introduced above, that only acts after a congestion already happened, the sliding window flow control mechanism is inherently a congestion avoidance mechanism.

Every target connection endpoint at the PGA Client and PGA Server Core will reserve a certain amount of buffer space (depicted as B_1 and B_2 in figure 4.18).

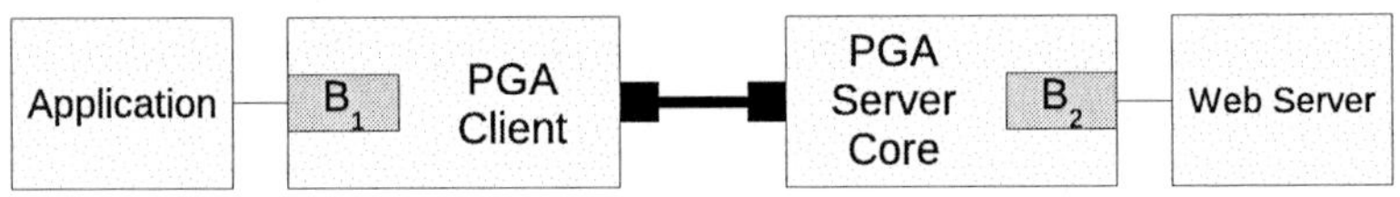

Figure 4.18: Target connection buffers

The initial size of B_1 and B_2 must be announced via `BUFFER_SIZE` messages when establishing the tunnel.

When reading the first data package from the application, the PGA Client must not read more data than B_2, the buffer size of the PGA Server Core. When reading the second data package, the PGA Client must determine again the amount of data it is allowed to read and forward. For this purpose it must subtract the data volume of the first data package (that has already been read and forwarded) from B_2. This *reading window* indicates an allowed number of bytes that the PGA Client may transmit before receiving further permission. The reading window of the PGA Client must be enlarged when the PGA Server Core successfully writes data to the web server. Therefore, the PGA Server Core must somehow communicate the number of written bytes to the PGA Client. TCP uses a positive acknowledgement (ACK) field in every TCP header. To save bandwidth, this ACK is delayed in many TCP implementations and "piggybacked" with normal payload packages. This saves some bandwidth but at the cost of maintaining a timed task that sends the ACK packages after a time-out when there are no payload packages to send. If normal packages are being sent while the timed task is waiting, the task has to be canceled. If this mechanism is used for the PGA tunnel protocol, timed tasks are created and canceled for every PGA tunnel in a very high frequency. Therefore this mechanism should only be used when the platform provides a low-overhead, high-performance timing framework so that the small amount of saved bandwidth is not bought with many computing resources.

If the number of read and transferred bytes is t and the number of bytes written at the opposite side and acknowledged is a then the size of the reading window w can always be determined by the following equation:

$$w = B_2 - t + a \tag{4.1}$$

If both PGA components adhere to this specification $t \leq a$ applies always. Insertion in the above equation leads to:

$$\begin{aligned} t &= B_2 + a - w \\ B_2 + a - w &\geq a \\ B_2 &\geq w \end{aligned} \tag{4.2}$$

This shows that when using the sliding window mechanism, the reading window on the PGA Client side is never larger than the buffer B_2 on the PGA Server Core side. Therefore, if the PGA Server Core receives a `DATA` message that results in an incomplete write operation and a buffer size that overflows B_2 it may assume that the PGA Client is compromised and may terminate the tunnel connection.

One challenge when using the sliding window mechanism is to utilize the available bandwidth of network connections with a large capacity (*bandwidth· delay*, see figure

4.7). When the size of B_2 is too small it may happen that the reading window at the PGA Client closes without any real congestion at the PGA Server Core happening. This is always the case when the difference between transferred and acknowledged data is as large as the buffer on the other side ($t - a = B_2$).

There is a mechanism for dynamic adjustment of sliding window sizes, described in [19]. Simply speaking, it works by constantly measuring the round-trip-time and the bandwidth of the connection. These both values can be used to calculate the needed window size for the current connection. If this value gets close to the currently used window size it is a sign that the window size is too small and it will be enlarged.

There are several ways to measure the bandwidth of a connection. In this case, passively measuring the tunnel throughput without special probe packages is suitable. So that the measurement has a high agility (changes are quickly detected) only the last window of the traffic, with a limited size, must be taken into consideration.

The algorithm to measure the tunnel bandwidth b can be very simple:

1. store the current time in a variable t_0
2. receive messages and add up the received data volume of all messages v until a certain limit (package count, received data volume or time-out) is reached
3. store the current time in a variable t_1
4. $b = \frac{v}{t_1 - t_0}$
5. repeat

A simple mechanism for measuring the round trip time of a tunnel is to send special `RTT` packages that must be instantly acknowledged with an `RTT_ACK` message when received. Because round trip time variation is normally low, an algorithm that backs off the sampling period should be used, starting with a sampling period s_0 up to a maximal sampling period s_{max}. For the dynamic window size scaling algorithm the shortest observed round trip time RTT_{min} should be used.

This way every PGA component could execute the following simple algorithm to efficiently measure the round trip time:

1. sampling period $s = s_0$

2. store the current time in a variable t_0

3. send an `RTT` package

4. upon receipt of an `RTT_ACK` message, store the current time in a variable t_1

5. $RTT_{min} = min(RTT_{min}, t_1 - t_0)$

6. wait for $s = min(2s, s_{max})$

7. goto 2

The round trip time measurement mechanism of TCP also accounts round trip time variation. It is needed for fine tuning of retransmission of packets that have not been acknowledged. Because there are no lost packages in a PGA tunnel, it is here not necessary to take round trip time variation into consideration.

Whenever the bandwidth b and the minimum round trip time RTT_{min} is measured, the necessary window size w can be calculated as follows:

$$w = \frac{b \cdot RTT_{min}}{2} \tag{4.3}$$

The following formula may be used to resize the local buffer size B after every calculation of w:

$$B = \begin{cases} B & w \leq \frac{B}{2} \\ 2B & w > \frac{B}{2} \end{cases} \tag{4.4}$$

This way the local buffer size doubles, whenever the measured necessary window size is half as large as the real buffer size.

If B changes, another `BUFFER_SIZE` message must be send through the tunnel so that the other PGA component can enlarge its reading window to fully utilize the available bandwidth.

Even if the sliding window flow control mechanism is used, the following attack can be executed to fill up as much buffer space at the PGA Server Core as possible: An adversary starts two software components, a sender and a receiver. The sender uses the PGA infrastructure to connect to the receiver. After establishing the connection, the adversary delays `RTT_ACK` messages on purpose, so that the PGA Server Core measures very long round trip times. This way the PGA Server Core will enlarge its local buffer size. After receiving a `BUFFER_SIZE` message with a very large number the adversary suddenly sends as much data as possible.

To fend off this attack, the PGA Server Core must define a maximum round trip time RTT_{max}, that will be used to calculate the window size. If a measured round trip time is larger than RTT_{max}, the PGA Server Core may assume that the PGA peer is compromised and may terminate the tunnel connection.

In summary, the sliding window flow control mechanism is very sophisticated, but constantly uses up bandwidth and computing resources.

Conclusion

The request/reply flow control mechanism is very simple to implement. But its inefficiency stands in direct opposition to the design goal of high performance for the PGA architecture. Therefore this flow control mechanism is not used.

The `XON/XOFF` flow control mechanism is also very simple to implement and has the advantage that the maximum bandwidth of the peer-to-peer connection can be used without any additional protocol mechanisms. The drawback is, that some very rare worst case scenarios are not handled very well.

The simplified sliding window flow control mechanism does not share the problems of the worst case scenario in the `XON/XOFF` flow control mechanism. But this small advantage comes at a high price. The protocol is substantially more complex and constantly uses bandwidth and computing resources.

Consequently, after evaluating the three flow control mechanisms above, `XON/XOFF` is used for the PGA tunneling protocol. This is an optimistic trade-off in favor of simplicity and performance to the disadvantage of complexity.

Verification

When using the `XON/XOFF` flow control mechanism, every PGA tunnel connection must keep track of both the local and remote states.

The state machine for local states is shown in figure 4.19 and has the following states:

On Data may be read from the target system and forwarded through the tunnel and data coming from the tunnel may be forwarded to the target system.

Off No more data must be read from the target system. Data coming from the tunnel may still be forwarded to the target system.

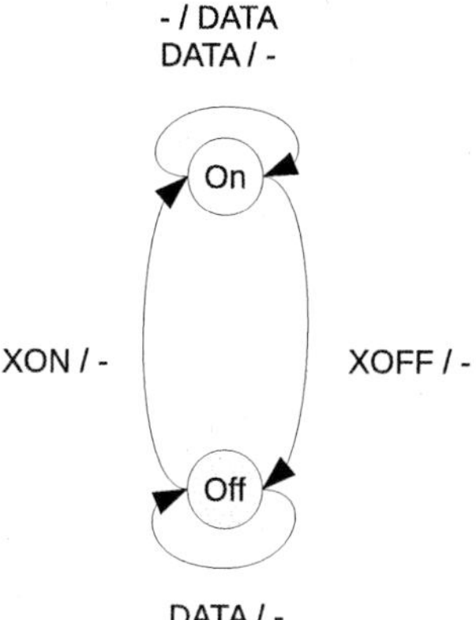

Figure 4.19: State machine for local `XON/XOFF` flow control

The remote states are the states the opposite side of a tunnel is expected to be in. In addition to the both local states described above the state machine for remote states shown in figure 4.20 has one additional state:

Emergency (shown as `E` in figure 4.20) No more data must be read from the tunnel. Data may still be read from the target system and forwarded through the tunnel.

There are state transitions where no messages are sent or received:

- `E` → `E`

  A local write operation occurred but the buffer size is still larger than the emergency limit.

- `E` → `Off`

  A local write operation occurred. The buffer size is now smaller than the the emergency limit but still larger than the limit for sending the `XOFF` message.

For creating a `ProMeLa` model, the local and remote state machines must be multiplied. Figure 4.21 shows a simplified product of both state machines. The state labels show the local state in the first line and the remote state in the second

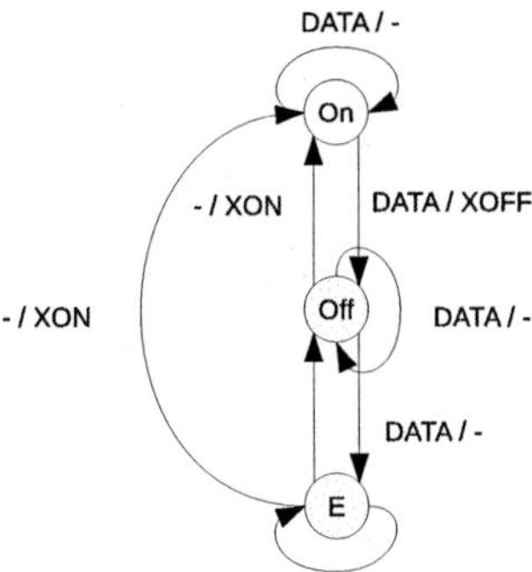

Figure 4.20: State machine for remote XON/XOFF flow control

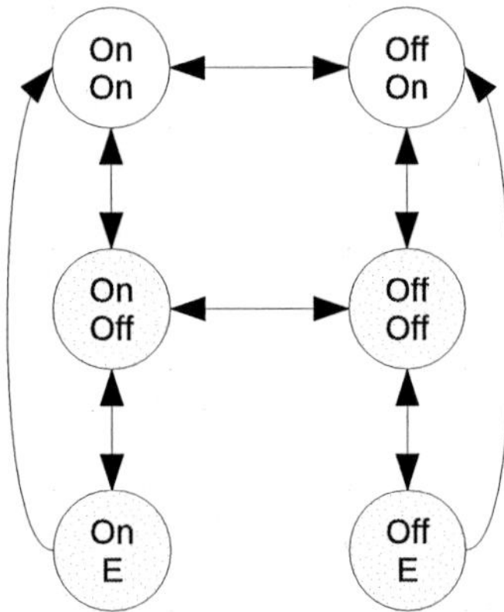

Figure 4.21: State machine for complete XON/XOFF flow control

line. For purposes of clarity, the transition details have been omitted but can be found in the source code of the ProMeLa model in section A.2 on page 197.

With the following command:

```
spin -c <promela_file>
```

the system modeled within the specified ProMeLa file is simulated. In this case the simulation of the XON/XOFF flow control is running endlessly as there is no final state in the model to be reached.

The model was verified with Spin:

```
(Spin Version 4.2.9 -- 8 February 2007)
        + Partial Order Reduction

Full statespace search for:
        never claim             - (none specified)
        assertion violations    +
        acceptance   cycles     - (not selected)
        invalid end states      +

State-vector 48 byte, depth reached 1575, errors: 0
    4224 states, stored
    9550 states, matched
   13774 transitions (= stored+matched)
       0 atomic steps
hash conflicts: 51 (resolved)

2.724   memory usage (Mbyte)

unreached in proctype :init:
        (0 of 3 states)
unreached in proctype PGA_Component
        line 61, state 62, "-end-"
        (1 of 62 states)
```

Spin did not report any errors, deadlocks or time-outs but some unreachable states in the processes "init" and "PGA_Component". This is again because there is no final state in this model to be reached and is not considered a problem.

Local flow control

Motivation

Connections to target systems (applications on the PGA Client side or web servers at the PGA Server Core side) are almost always faster than the tunnel connection between a PGA Client and a PGA Server Core. Therefore another buffer in front of the tunnel at both the PGA Client and the PGA Server Core side is needed (see figure 4.22).

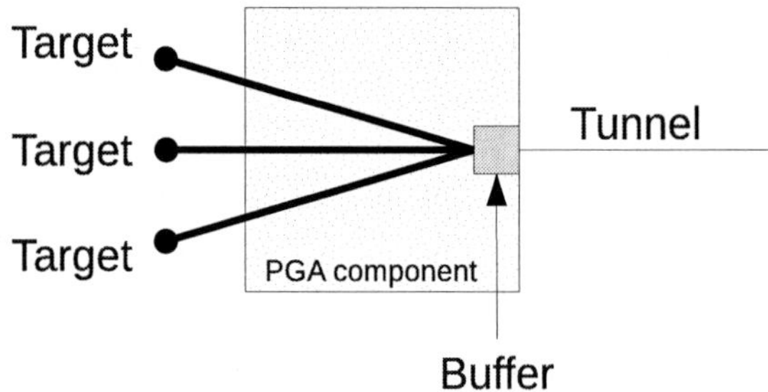

Figure 4.22: Tunnel buffer at a PGA component

Because this buffer must also be protected against data overflow, in addition to a working end-to-end flow control mechanism, another flow control mechanism for local data forwarding is needed.

Design

If the buffer size reaches a certain threshold size, the PGA Client or PGA Server Core must stop reading new data from the target connections. If the buffer size falls below the threshold, the PGA components must resume reading and forwarding new data from the target connections.

There are at least two strategies stop and restart the target connections:

1. Stop all target connections at once when the buffer reaches the threshold size and continue reading and forwarding new data at all target connections when the buffer size falls below the threshold.

2. Stop single target connections one after the other when they try passing data through the tunnel and the buffer threshold size is reached. Store the stopped target connections into a list. Restart all target connections in this list when the buffer size falls below the threshold.

Both strategies have their advantages and disadvantages:

Strategy 1 minimizes buffer space usage but wastes computing resources by stopping and restarting connections that maybe never had produced any data during the time the buffer size was larger than the threshold value.

Strategy 2 minimizes computing resources by only stopping connections that produced new data during the time the buffer size was larger than the threshold value but wastes buffer space as each of these connections may still add some data to the buffer despite already being larger than the threshold value. In addition to that some memory is used for the list that holds the references to the connections that have been stopped and must be restarted when the buffer size falls below the threshold.

The current PGA implementation uses strategy 1 because of the following reasons:

- The number of target connections at a single tunnel is equivalent to the concurrent connections of one single PGA Client. The intended main usage of the PGA Client is a local proxy for one single user. The PGA Client could also be used as an anonymizing proxy for a whole Intranet user group, but this scenario is probably rare. Therefore the number of target connections is (most of the time) very small.

- Stopping connections is not a very computationally intensive task.

- The main idea of the local flow control mechanism is to protect the tunnel buffer from overflows, not to minimize computational resources.

Because the local flow control mechanism (like the name already suggests) has no dependencies on the PGA component at the other side of the tunnel, it is perfectly valid if different implementations of PGA components use different local flow control mechanisms on both sides of a tunnel. Therefore, a full specification of this mechanism is not necessary.

4.6.5 Adaptive dummy traffic generation

The PGA Client has to send a constant data stream padded with dummy traffic to the PGA Server Core to protect the user against traffic analysis attacks. The PGA Client does not know how much user data every *other* member of its anonymity group has to send at a certain point in time. Requesting this information constantly from every other member before sending a message would cost a lot of bandwidth and latency. Therefore the PGA Client always fills up the messages with dummy traffic up to its standard size l_s (see Figure 4.23).

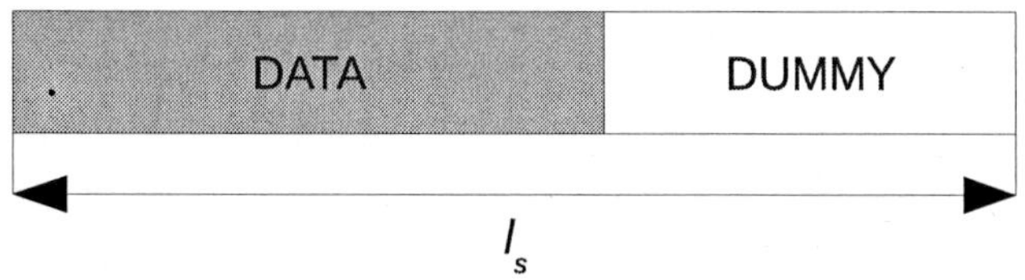

Figure 4.23: PGA Client dummy traffic generation

The PGA Server Core also has to send a constant data stream to all PGA Clients which joined an anonymity group (the package size and delay are depending on every single anonymity group properties). But, in contrast to the PGA Client, the PGA Server Core knows exactly how much user data is available when a batch of messages must be sent to the PGA Clients. This information could be used to save bandwidth by adapting the message size for every batch:

Before sending a batch of messages for an anonymity group, the PGA Server Core has to find the maximum of available user data for all PGA Clients in this anonymity group, $l_{max} \leq l_s$. It can stop processing, if a PGA Client has the maximum amount of user data available (the standard message size l_s). After finding the maximum available user data, the PGA Server Core has to send a message with the size l_{max} to all PGA Clients of the anonymity group (see Figure 4.24).

If the number of PGA Clients in an anonymity group is n and the delay between sending packages is Δt, the saved bandwidth Δb(compared to the simple approach where the PGA Server Core always sends messages with the size l_s) is:

$\Delta b = \frac{n \cdot (l_s - l_{max})}{\Delta t}$

There is an interesting effect in this equation: if n gets larger, Δb does not

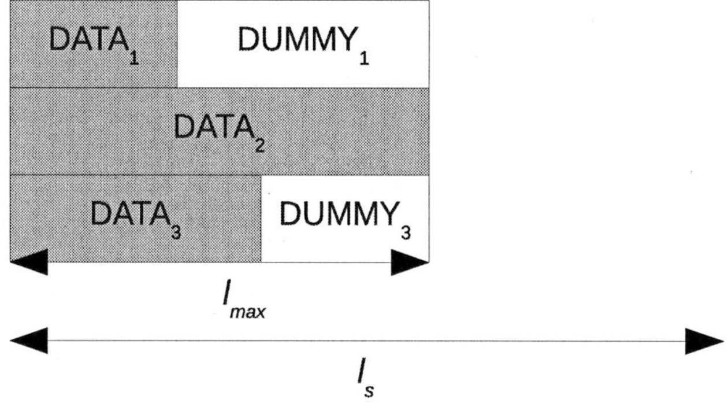

Figure 4.24: Adaptive dummy traffic generation at PGA Server Core

automatically get larger, because the probability for $l_{max} \leq l_s$ becomes smaller with a larger n. Therefore, the exact value of Δb depends on the traffic characteristics of all anonymity group members.

Adaptive dummy traffic generation is a very simple operation concerning computational resources that can save a lot of valuable bandwidth (under certain conditions), but unfortunately, it also opens up the possibility of hidden channels: Compromised applications could enforce l_{max} for certain amounts of time and transmit sensitive information via modulation of these time periods. Interesting to note is that the larger the saved bandwidth Δb is, the larger is the available bandwidth for a hidden channel. Because hidden channels are a severe security risk, adaptive dummy traffic generation is *not* used in the PGA architecture.

4.7 Remote Management protocol

The Remote Management protocol is used for exchanging management information between the PGA Remote Management and the PGA Server.

The Remote Management protocol must enable the following functions for the PGA Remote Management:

PGA Server Core status shows if the PGA Server Core is running or not

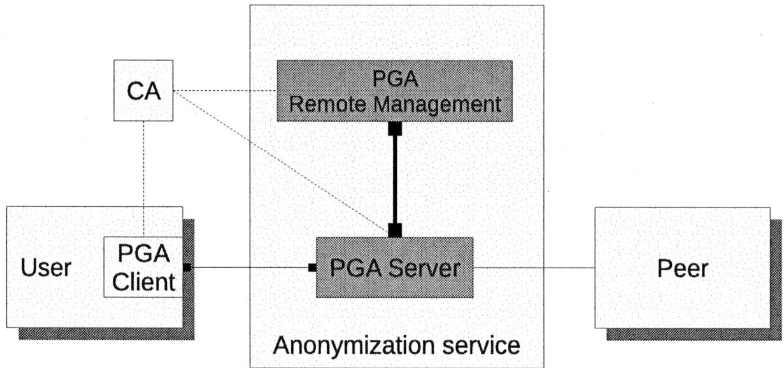

Figure 4.25: Remote Management

Number of PGA Clients shows the number of PGA Clients connected to the PGA Server Core

Remaining data volume shows the remaining data volume that is available for anonymous users

Anonymity groups information shows a list of all anonymity groups including information about the upstream and downstream packet stream definitions (message size and delay) and the current size of the anonymity group

Anonymity group configuration provides means to add, edit, remove and re-order the anonymity groups of a PGA Server Core

Service start provides means to start the PGA Server Core service (to accept and serve requests from PGA Clients)

Service stop provides means to stop the PGA Server Core service

Key pair generation provides means to generate a key pair for the PGA Server Core

Certificate Request generation provides means to generate a certificate request for the PGA Server Core that can be send to the PGA Certificate Authority

Certificate verification provides means to verify a certificate and show the verification result

Certificate import provides means to import a certificate from the PGA Certificate authority

Certificate information shows the selected certificate of the PGA Server Core

Service port information shows the selected service port (the port where to accept and serve requests from PGA Clients) of the PGA Server Core

Service port configuration provides means to set the service port of the PGA Server Core

Log level information shows the currently selected log level of the PGA Server Cores

Log level configuration provides means to set the log level of the PGA Server Core

Data retention information shows if the PGA Server Core uses data retention

Data retention configuration provides means to switch data retention at PGA Server Core on or off

Data retention period information shows the data retention period of the PGA Server Core

Data retention period configuration provides means to set the PGA Server Core data retention period

Data retention filtering information shows if a filter is used for the PGA Server Core data retention

Data retention filtering configuration provides means to configure a filter for the PGA Server Core data retention

Data retention encryption information shows if encryption is used for the PGA Server Core data retention

Data retention encryption configuration provides means to configure an ID for PGA Server Core data retention encryption

Data retention rotation information shows the data retention rotation period of the PGA Server Core

Data retention rotation configuration provides means to set the PGA Server Core data retention rotation period

Anonymous users policy information shows the policy (bandwidth, data volume) for anonymous users at the PGA Server Core

Anonymous users policy configuration provides means to set the policy for anonymous users at the PGA Server Core

Firewall information shows the firewall rules of the PGA Server Core (list of internal networks)

Firewall configuration provides means to add, edit, remove and reorder internal networks of the PGA Server Core

Statistical information shows statistical information about the used bandwidth, the number of connected PGA Clients, the CPU load and the system memory usage for different time periods (last hour, day, week, month, year)

The initial version of the Remote Management protocol was using a simple protocol with length prefixed message frames, a type header and bodies with XML elements. The corresponding PGA Remote Management was implemented as a standalone Swing based application.

Shortly after finishing the first prototype implementation based on this initial Remote Management protocol version, Java version 5.0 was released with beginning support for Java Management Extensions (JMX) [44], a technology for managing and monitoring applications[12]. JMX was significantly enhanced with Java version 6.0[13]. Because JMX as a standard part of Java offers many benefits compared to a proprietary solution, the initial version of the Remote Management protocol was

[12]`http://docs.oracle.com/javase/1.5.0/docs/guide/jmx/`, last visited: January 2012

[13]`http://docs.oracle.com/javase/6/docs/technotes/guides/jmx/enhancements.html`, last visited: January 2012

discontinued and it was based on JMX instead. Implementation details can be found in section 6.5 on page 155.

Chapter 5

Java NIO Framework

5.1 Motivation

The PGA architecture works with several different TCP connections. These TCP connection have to have a good performance and they have to be scalable. Otherwise it would be impossible to create large anonymity groups (one significant property of good anonymization) with the PGA architecture. In addition to the performance requirement, the data on all these TCP connections has to be buffered, forwarded, framed, unframed, encrypted, decrypted, converted, ...

Because this functionality was needed for all components of the PGA architecture, a reusable framework with all the properties described above was needed. Unfortunately, at the time of implementing the PGA architecture, such a framework was non-existent and therefore created as a part of this work.

5.2 Introduction

For many years, the performance of CPU's improved according to Moore's law [39] (see Figure 5.1). Because Moore's law cannot be sustained indefinitely and transistors slowly reach the limits of miniaturization, parallelization is used to increase the performance of computers. Multi-core and many-core processing units are now becoming the standard in computing architectures. The expected growth in number of cores per unit is a challenge for software engineers in almost all fields.

Java network application programmers have two basic choices:

- use the classical I/O API (Streams, blocking I/O)

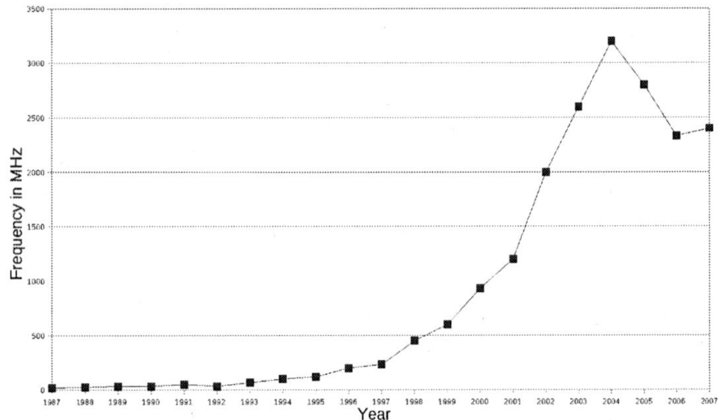

Figure 5.1: Clock rate history of Intel-CPU's (data source: Wikipedia)

- use the NIO API (ByteBuffers, non-blocking I/O)

The classical I/O API is very easy to use, even for network connections secured with SSL. Because it uses blocking I/O, the *one thread per socket* multiplexing strategy must be used to serve several network connections. Even though this API scales with the number of available cores, the runtime performance of network applications using this API is very poor.

The NIO API provides mechanisms for non-blocking I/O. With non-blocking I/O it becomes possible to use *readiness selection* as the multiplexing strategy for serving several network connections. On the other hand, programming with the NIO API is very difficult. A whole book has been written about it [25]. If attention is paid to all the necessary NIO details, a programmer must write a lot of so-called boilerplate code, even for the most simple network application. The complexity is increased many times if NIO is combined with SSL for secure network connections or support for high-performance, parallel systems. Many of these challenges and their proposed solutions are described in [45].

The Java NIO Framework is an extensible programming library that solves many problems that Java network application programmers face when using the original NIO library:

- In contrast to the original NIO library the Java NIO Framework has a very simple API, hiding all unnecessary details.
- Support for securing network connections with SSL is an integral part of the library instead of providing a separate, add-on engine.
- The I/O processing performance of network applications using the Java NIO Framework automatically scales with the number of available cores.

Work on the Java NIO Framework was started after Ron Hitchen's presentation "How to Build a Scalable Multiplexed Server With NIO" at the JavaOne Conference 2006 [26]. Although there have been other frameworks available, e.g. [36, 2, 51, 55], none of them had the envisioned scalability and ease of use. The Java NIO Framework has been published in August 2007 and is available at `http://nioframework.sourceforge.net`[1]. It is Free Software released under the GNU Lesser General Public License[2] version 3.

[1]last visited: January 2012

[2]`http://www.gnu.org/licenses/gpl.html`, last visited: January 2012

5.3 Multiplexing Strategies

Two multiplexing strategies were mentioned in the introduction, *one thread per socket* and *readiness selection*. In the next sections both strategies are briefly introduced and analyzed.

5.3.1 One Thread Per Socket

Threads are a mechanism to split a process into several simultaneously running tasks. Threads differ from normal processes by sharing memory and other resources. Therefore they are often called lightweight processes. Switching between threads is typically faster than switching between processes.

When a server uses the *one thread per socket* multiplexing strategy it creates one thread for every client connection. When executing blocking I/O operations the thread is also blocked until the operation completes its execution (e.g. when trying to read data from a socket the thread blocks until new data is available to read from the socket).

This strategy is very simple to implement because every thread just continues its operation after returning from a blocking operation and all internal states of the thread are automatically restored. A programmer can implement the thread (more or less) as if the server handles only one client connection.

The drawback of this multiplexing strategy is that it does not scale well. Each blocked thread acts as a socket monitor and the thread scheduler is the notification mechanism. Neither of them was designed for such a purpose.

A remaining problem of this strategy is that a design with massive parallel threads naturally is prone to typical threading problems, e.g. deadlocks, lifelocks and starvation.

5.3.2 Readiness Selection

Readiness selection is a multiplexing strategy that enables a server to handle many client connections simultaneously with a single thread. An overview of readiness selection is given in [32] when presenting the reactor design pattern.

The reactor design pattern proposes the software architecture presented in Figure 5.2.

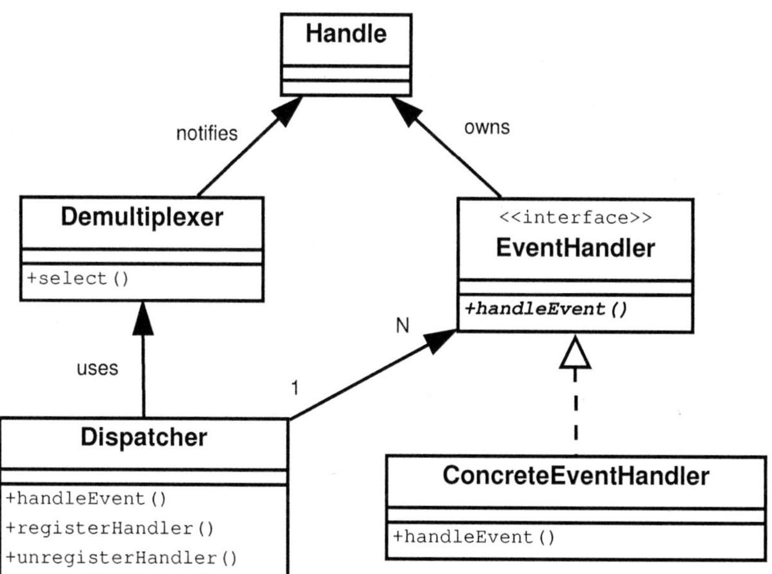

Figure 5.2: Reactor design pattern

- The class `Handle` identifies resources that are managed by an operating system, e.g. sockets.
- The class `Demultiplexer` blocks awaiting events to occur on a set of `Handles`. It returns when it is possible to initiate an operation on a `Handle` without blocking. The method `select()` returns which `Handles` can have operations invoked on them synchronously without blocking the application process.
- The class `Dispatcher` defines an interface for registering, removing, and dispatching `EventHandlers`. Ultimately, the `Demultiplexer` is responsible for waiting until new events occur. When it detects new events, it informs the `Dispatcher` to call back application-specific event handlers.
- The interface `EventHandler` specifies a hook method that abstractly represents the dispatching operation for service-specific events.
- The class `ConcreteEventHandler` implements the hook method as well as the methods to process these events in an application-specific manner. Applications register `ConcreteEventHandlers` with the `Dispatcher` to process certain types of events. When these events arrive, the `Dispatcher` calls back the hook method of the appropriate `ConcreteEventHandler`.

Readiness selection scales much better but it is not as easy to implement as the *one thread per socket* strategy.

5.4 Java NIO Framework Design

Because the Java NIO Framework should be scalable to handle thousands of network connections simultaneously, the decision was made to use *readiness selection* as the multiplexing strategy, which is much more appropriate for high-performance I/O than the *one thread per socket* strategy.

5.4.1 Mapping the Reactor Design Pattern

If the reactor design pattern presented above had been used for the Java NIO Framework without modification, every application-specific ConcreteEventHandler would still have to take care of many NIO specific details. These include buffers, queues, incomplete write operations, encryption of data streams and much more. To provide a simple API to Java network application programmers, the Java NIO Framework was complemented with several additional helper classes and interfaces that will be introduced in the following sections.

The concepts and techniques used to design and implement a safe and scalable framework that effectively exploits multiple processors are presented in [43].

A simplified model of the Java NIO Framework core is shown in Figure 5.3.

The gray UML elements (`Runnable`, `Thread`, `Selector`, `SelectionKey` and `Executor`) are part of the Java Development Kit (JDK). The interface `Runnable` and the class `Thread` were part of JDK from the very beginning, `Selector` and `SelectionKey` have been added to the JDK with the NIO package in JDK v1.4 and the interface `Executor` was added with the concurrency package (`java.util.concurrent.*`) in JDK v1.5. The white UML elements (`ChannelHandler`, `AbstractChannelHandler`, `HandlerAdapter` and `Dispatcher`) are the essential core classes of the Java NIO Framework.

The `Dispatcher` is a `Thread` that runs in an endless loop, processes registrations of `ChannelHandlers` with a channel (a nexus for I/O operations that represents an open connection to an entity such as a network socket) and uses an `Executor` to offload the execution of selected `HandlerAdapters` (see Figure 5.4 for the corresponding sequence diagram). The `Executor` interface hides the mechanics of how each task will be executed, including details of thread use, scheduling, etc. This abstraction is necessary because the Java NIO Framework may be used on a wide range of systems, from low-cost embedded devices up to high-performance multi-core servers.

The abstract class `Selector` determines which registered channels are ready.

The abstract class `SelectionKey` associates a channel with a `Selector`, tells the `Selector` which events to monitor for the channel and holds a reference to an arbitrary object, called "attachment". In the current architecture the attachment is a `HandlerAdapter`.

The `EventHandler` from the reactor design pattern is split up into several components. The first component is the class `HandlerAdapter`. When it is executed, it manages all the operations on a channel (connect, read, write, close) and its queues, interacts with the `Dispatcher` and `SelectionKey` classes and, most importantly, hides and encapsulates most NIO details from higher level classes and interfaces

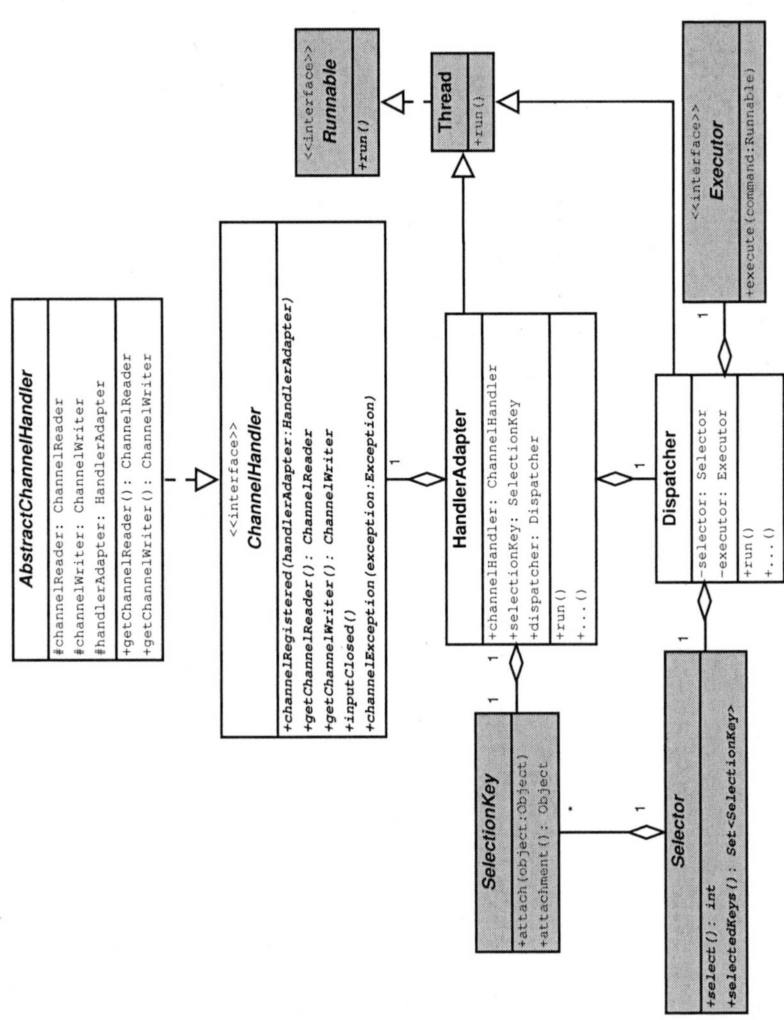

Figure 5.3: Simplified Java NIO Framework Core

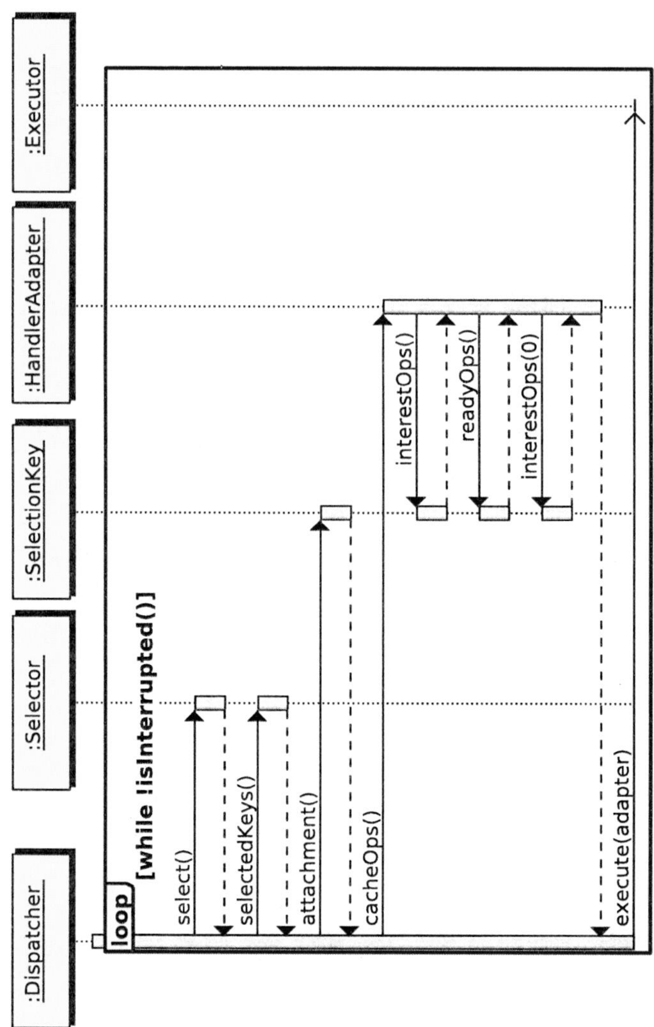

Figure 5.4: Sequence diagram of Dispatcher main loop

(see Figure 5.5 for the corresponding sequence diagram).

The second EventHandler component in the Java NIO Framework is the interface ChannelHandler. It defines the methods that any application-specific channel handler class has to implement so that it can be used in the Java NIO framework. These include:

```
public void channelRegistered(
        HandlerAdapter handlerAdapter)
```

This method gets called when a channel was registered at the Dispatcher. It is mostly used on server type applications to send a welcome message to clients that just connected.

```
public ChannelReader getChannelReader()
```

This method returns the ChannelReader that will be used by the HandlerAdapter, if there is data to be read from the channel.

```
public ChannelWriter getChannelWriter()
```

This method returns the ChannelWriter that will be used by the HandlerAdapter, if there is data to be written to the channel.

```
public void inputClosed()
```

This method gets called by the HandlerAdapter, if no more data can be read from the ChannelReader.

```
public void channelException(Exception exception)
```

The HandlerAdapter calls this method, if an exception occurred while reading from or writing to the channel.

The abstract class AbstractChannelHandler provides a simple base for implementing all the application specific ChannelHandlers (not shown in Figure 5.3). It uses the standard Java NIO Framework ChannelReader, ChannelWriter and HandlerAdapter and already implements the methods channelRegistered(HandlerAdapter handlerAdapter), getChannelReader() and

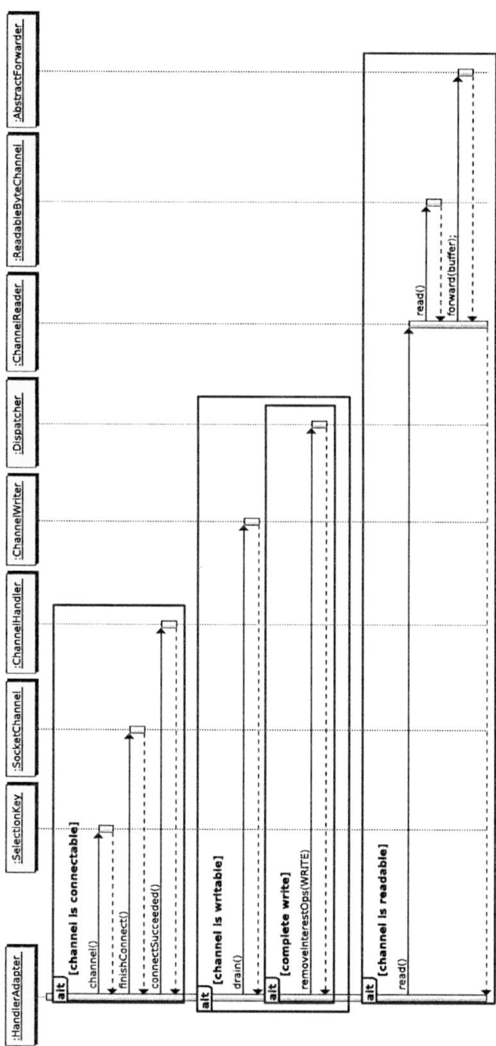

Figure 5.5: Sequence diagram of HandlerAdapter execution

`getChannelWriter()`. Most application specific `ChannelHandlers` will probably extend `AbstractChannelHandler` but application developers also have the freedom to provide a completely different implementation of the `ChannelHandler` interface.

The `ConcreteEventHandler` of the reactor design pattern is represented by these application specific `ChannelHandlers`.

Table 5.1 shows the mappings from the reactor design pattern to the Java NIO Framework.

Table 5.1: Mappings from reactor design pattern to the Java NIO Framework

Reactor Design Pattern	Java NIO Framework
Dispatcher	Dispatcher
Demultiplexer	Selector
Handle	SelectionKey
EventHandler	HandlerAdapter ChannelHandler AbstractChannelHandler Executor
ConcreteEventHandler	n.a.

5.4.2 Example

The following simple example shows how the core elements of the Java NIO Framework interact:

A client system is using the Java NIO Framework to read some data from a server system. The client application has a class `ClientChannelHandler` which extends the abstract class `AbstractChannelHandler`. The following operational sequence is necessary:

1. The client system connects to the server system with the classic I/O mechanisms, e.g. with the `java.net.Socket` class and gets the Channel "channel" from the socket.

2. The client creates an instance "handler" of `ClientChannelHandler` and calls

```
Dispatcher.registerChannel(channel, handler)
```

3. The `Dispatcher` registers the channel at the `Selector`, which creates a `SelectionKey`. A new `HandlerAdapter` is created and attached to the `SelectionKey`. The `HandlerAdapter` asks the handler for its `ChannelReader` and `ChannelWriter`. The last step is to call

   ```
   handler.channelRegistered(handlerAdapter)
   ```

   so that the client application may execute initial actions, e.g. send some initial data to the server.

4. The server application sends some data to the client application.

5. `Selector` returns from `select()` because there is readable data on the channel.

6. The `Dispatcher` gets the list of selected keys via `Selector.selectedKeys()` and gets the `HandlerAdapter` of every selected `SelectionKey` via `SelectionKey.attachment()`. The method `cacheOps()` of every returned `HandlerAdapter` is called to cache the current operations of interest (connect, read, write, ...) and clear all operations of interest from the `SelectionKey` so that the channel does not get selected anymore from the `Selector` until the `HandlerAdapter` is done with handling the current selection. The `HandlerAdapter` execution is offloaded from the `Dispatcher` thread by calling `Executor.execute(handlerAdapter)`.

7. Depending on many factors (the execution strategy of the client application, the system load, etc.) the `HandlerAdapter` will be executed after some time. It reads data from the channel by calling `ChannelReader.read()` and processes this new data according to the purpose of the application (e.g. output to console, forward to another application, echo back to the server, etc.). Most application specific `ChannelHandlers` will provide this funcionality by creating a customized hierarchy of Java NIO Framework forwarders and transformers (see section 5.4.4).

5.4.3 Parallelization

Some parts of the Java NIO Framework are parallelized by default, other parts can be customized to be parallelized.

Execution

The execution of all `HandlerAdapters` is off-loaded from the `Dispatcher` thread to an `Executor`. Because I/O operations are typically short-lived asynchronous tasks, the default `Executor` of the Java NIO Framework uses a thread pool that creates new threads as needed, but will reuse previously constructed threads when they are available. Threads that have not been used for a while are terminated and removed from the pool. Therefore, if the `Executor` remains idle for long enough, it will not consume any resources.

Not every I/O operation meets the typical criteria, e.g. SSL operations are comparatively long-lived. If the actual requirements (e.g. a certain thread usage or scheduling) are not met by the default Java NIO Framework `Executor`, it can be customized with the method `Dispatcher.setExecutor()`. Because this method is thread-safe, the `Executor` can even be hot-swapped at runtime.

Selection

There is only *one* `Dispatcher` running per default in the Java NIO Framework, waiting until new events occur on channels represented by `SelectionKeys`. If the `Dispatcher` would ever become the bottleneck of the framework it could simply be parallelized by starting several `Dispatcher` instances.

Load-balancing could be done by distributing channel registrations between the parallel `Dispatcher` instances. Some of the most simple scheduling algorithms that could be applied are round-robin distribution or random scheduling.

If connection lifetimes have a high degree of variation, both algorithms could lead to a very unequal distribution of channels to `Dispatchers`. To prevent this scenario, an *active channel* counter could be integrated into every `Dispatcher` and a *lowest-channel-counter-first* scheduling algorithm could be used.

If connections have a high degree of "activity" variation, i.e. on some channels there is always something to read or write and other channels are mostly idle, the scheduling algorithm should be based on a `select()`-counter in the `Dispatcher`.

Accepting

Another thread, the `Acceptor`, is running on server type applications. It is listening on a server socket for incoming connection requests from clients over the network.

Every time a request comes in, the `Acceptor` creates a new channel and appropriate handler, and registers them both at the `Dispatcher` of the server type application (or `Dispatchers`, if selection was parallelized like mentioned in Section 5.4.3).

Currently the Java NIO Framework does not support parallelization of `Acceptors`.

5.4.4 I/O Processing

When application data units (objects, messages, etc.) have to be transmitted over a TCP network connection, they have to be transformed into a serialized representation of bytes.

There are many ways to represent application data and there are also many ways to serialize data into a byte stream. Therefore, there are countless transformations between application space and network space imaginable.

The first approach to this problem in the Java NIO Framework was to provide an extensible hierarchy of classes, where every class dealt with a certain operation (e.g. buffering, string serialization, SSL encryption). This architecture turned out to be very simple and efficient (only one lock per class). The downside of this approach was that every combination of operations required its own implementing class. Changing the order or composition of operations was very difficult and much too inflexible for a generic framework.

The second and current approach to message processing is *object composition*, where a set of `Forwarder` classes have been implemented and each class offers just a certain forwarding operation. A special subclass, `Transformer`, is used for all operations that actually *transform* data when processing.

An application programmer can put these `Forwarders` and `Transformers` together into a hierarchy of almost arbitrary order. Almost no programming effort is required besides assembling the needed classes of the processing hierarchy in the desired order.

The current approach, to favor object composition over class inheritance, has also been discussed in detail (and was recommended) in the seminal book "Design Patterns: Elements of Reusable Object-Oriented Software"[22].

A diagrammatic example of the I/O processing architecture is shown in Figure 5.6:

The shapes T_x are the transformation classes. When writing to a channel, the `ChannelHandler` hands the application level data units to one of the input transfor-

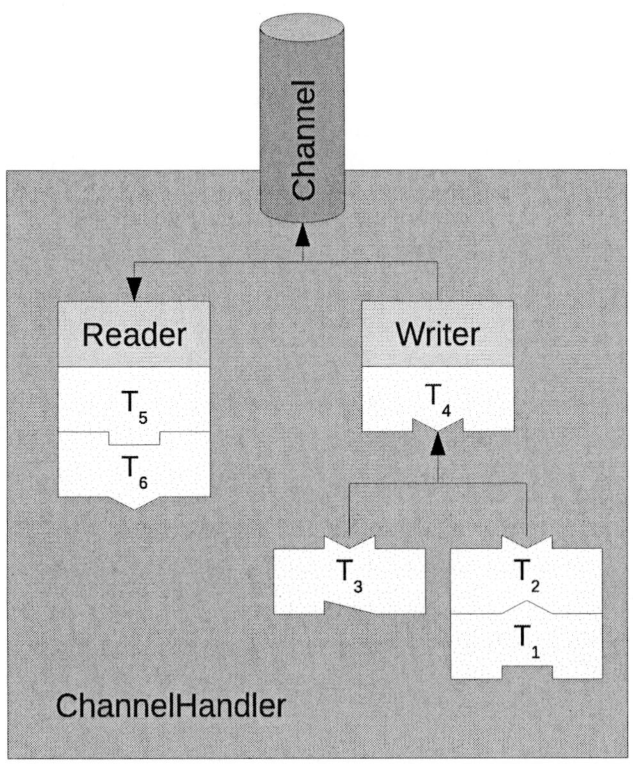

Figure 5.6: I/O processing example

mation classes T_1, T_2, T_3 or T_4 (depending on the type of input it just accepted). Every transformation class transforms the data and hands it over to its next transformer until it reaches the `ChannelWriter`, which writes the final byte stream to the channel and handles many channel specific problems, e.g. incomplete write operations.

When reading from a channel, the `CannelReader` handles the channel specific problems, e.g. connection closing and read buffer reallocations. After reading a byte stream from the Channel, the `CannelReader` passes the data to T_5, which transforms the data. The `ChannelHandler` can get the application level messages from T_6.

There are four basic I/O models for the transformation classes T_x. In ascending order of complexity they are:

- **1:1** (one type of input, one type of output)
- **1:N** (one type of input, different types of output)
- **N:1** (different types of input, one kind of output)
- **N:M** (different types of input, different types of output)

Every model is valid insofar as one can establish a fully functional transformation hierarchy with any of these I/O models. While the 1:1 model would be the most simple one, transformation classes of the N:M model would have the highest flexibility. The interesting thing to note here is that with respect to flexibility every transformation class of the more complex models can be replaced by chaining several transformation classes of the 1:1 model. While trying to implement prototypes for all models above it became clear that the most simple API was provided by using Java Generics[3] (also known as "parameterized types" in [22]) and the 1:1 model. Another advantage of the 1:1 model is the encouragement of code reuse, because every transformation should be implemented in a separate class.

The elegance and simplicity comes at the small price of an almost immeasurable performance loss. Currently, Java Generics are implemented by type erasure: generic type information is present only at compile time, after which it is erased by the compiler. The compiler automatically inserts cast operations into the byte code at necessary places which may cause a tiny performance loss. Using the 1:1 model

[3] `http://docs.oracle.com/javase/1.5.0/docs/guide/language/generics.html`, last visited: January 2012

results in slightly longer transformation chains, more involved objects and more locking and unlocking when passing data through a transformation hierarchy.

5.4.5 Synchronization of Parallel I/O

The first version of the Java NIO Framework was running with just one single thread. This had two very positive consequences:

- no thread synchronization issues (deadlocks, lifelocks, starvation, ...)
- no locking mechanism necessary

Both properties led to a very simple architecture with a very high performance on single processor systems. But at the same time a new trend was becoming the norm: multiple cores.

It was clear that full utilization of a multi-core system was impossible with a single-threaded framework. Therefore the Java NIO Framework was redesigned to its current variant.

The current version offloads the execution of `HandlerAdapters` to an `Executor`. This way it is possible to have several `HandlerAdapters` run simultaneously, using all available cores in a high-performance system. Unfortunately, this approach leads again to all known multithreading issues.

While offering a scalable framework it must also be ensured that data integrity is always guaranteed. While it is no problem when one thread reads from a channel while another thread is writing to the channel simultaneously, it must never happen that two threads are reading from or writing to the same channel at the same time. Both situations would lead to data corruption.

Clear, correct, robust and reusable techniques for synchronization of parallel threads in Java that can be used in the Java NIO framework are presented in [6].

Serialization of Read Operations

If a channel has new readable data, the call to `Selector.select()` returns and the `Dispatcher` calls `HandlerAdapter.cacheOps()` before offloading the execution of the `HandlerAdapter` to the `Executor`.

When the method `HandlerAdapter.cacheOps()` is called, it caches all current operation interests (read, write, ...) and removes all operation interests from the

SelectionKey. This way the channel does not get selected by the Selector anymore and all read operations on the channel are serialized.

When the HandlerAdapter gets executed by the Executor after some time, it restores the cached interest operations at the SelectionKey at the very end of its execution (sometimes also a different interest set, depending of the events that happened while the HandlerAdapter was executed). The channel will then be monitored and selected by the Selector again.

If reading from a channel does not happen intentionally outside the Java NIO Framework, all read operations on all channels are serialized.

Serialization of Write Operations

There are three situations when write operations at a channel may happen:

- A ChannelHandler reads some data from its channel and immediately produces and writes a response to the channel (e.g. a HTTP response after reading a HTTP request).
- The HandlerAdapter is executed and tries to drain a ChannelWriter that was filled because of a previous incomplete write operation.
- Another thread writes directly to a channel (e.g. into a specific SSL tunnel of a VPN application).

To serialize all these write operations, all ChannelWriter implementations must use a lock when writing data to the channel.

Because changing the set of operation interest (necessary e.g. when an incomplete write operation occurs) must be handled differently depending on whether the HandlerAdapter has already cached them or not, the HandlerAdapter must use another lock to protect all changes to the set of operation interests and its cache.

5.5 Forwarders and Transformers

The Java NIO Framework provides many useful Forwarders and Transformers to make the implementation of application specific ChannelHandlers as simple as possible.

5.5.1 Atomic Forwarders

Atomic `Forwarders` are the basic building blocks of the Java NIO Framework I/O processing. They do *not* consist of other `Forwarders`. Up to now, the following atomic `Forwarders` have been implemented:

ByteBufferToArrayTransformer

`Input :` `ByteBuffer`[4]
`Output:` `ByteBuffer[]`

The `ByteBufferToArrayTransformer` transforms a `ByteBuffer` into an array of `ByteBuffers`. The returned array contains only one single entry: the `ByteBuffer` provided as input. This way it is possible to use a `ByteBuffer` as input of a `Forwarder` that only accepts arrays of `ByteBuffers`.

ByteBufferArraySequenceForwarder

`Input :` `ByteBuffer[]`
`Output:` `ByteBuffer`

The `ByteBufferArraySequenceForwarder` forwards an array of `ByteBuffers` as a sequence of `ByteBuffers`. This way it is possible to convert an array of `ByteBuffers` so that it can be used as the input of a `Forwarder` that only accepts single `ByteBuffers`.

StringToByteBufferTransformer

`Input :` `String`
`Output:` `ByteBuffer`

The `StringToByteBufferTransformer` transforms a given `String` into a `ByteBuffer`. The transformation is controlled by a given charset (`java.nio.charset.Charset`). This is needed e.g. when transforming application messages into byte streams that can be transmitted over networks.

---

[4] `http://docs.oracle.com/javase/6/docs/api/java/nio/ByteBuffer.html`, last visited: January 2012

ByteBufferToStringTransformer

`Input :   String`
`Output:   ByteBuffer`

The `ByteBufferToStringTransformer` transforms a given `ByteBuffer` into a `String`. The transformation is controlled by a given charset (`java.nio.charset.Charset`). This is needed e.g. when transforming network byte streams back into application messages.

SplitStringForwarder

`Input :   String`
`Output:   String`

The `SplitStringForwarder` splits a `String` with a given delimiter into a sequence of `Strings`. This way it is possible to separate several adjacent messages from each other.

BufferForwarder

`Input :   ByteBuffer[]`
`Output:   ByteBuffer`

The `BufferForwarder` buffers input data *by copying* and can forward chunks of buffered data with a given or a maximum size. This way it can be used as a component for traffic shaping or processing dummy traffic. Several input `ByteBuffers` are copied into a single output `ByteBuffer`.

BufferArrayForwarder

`Input :   ByteBuffer[]`
`Output:   ByteBuffer[]`

The `BufferArrayForwarder` works similar to `BufferForwarder` above but buffers input data *by reference* and forwards data with a different output type (the input `ByteBuffers` are *not* copied and merged).

PrefixTransformer

`Input :   ByteBuffer[]`
`Output:   ByteBuffer[]`

The `PrefixTransformer` prefixes an array of `ByteBuffers` with another `ByteBuffer`. This is useful whenever data has to be marked with different types (e.g. to differentiate between *data* and *dummy* messages).

ChannelReader

`Input : Void`
`Output: ByteBuffer`

The `ChannelReader` is a special `Forwarder` that handles all necessary details (read buffer allocation, counters, read errors, ...) when reading data from a readable byte channel[5]. It passes the read data to the next `Forwarder` as a series of `ByteBuffers`. Because it is not possible to *write* any data to a `ReadableByteChannel`, the `ChannelReader` does not implement the `forward()` method.

ChannelWriter

`Input : ByteBuffer`
`Output: Void`

The `ChannelWriter` is a special `Forwarder` that handles all necessary details (incomplete write operations, counters, write errors, ...) when writing data to a writable byte channel[6]. It writes all input data to the channel. Because it is not possible to *read* any data from a `WritableByteChannel`, the `ChannelWriter` does not implement the `setNextForwarder()` method.

FramingInputForwarder

`Input : ByteBuffer`
`Output: ByteBuffer`

The `FramingInputForwarder` unframes length prefixed messages by evaluating and removing a length header. Input is stored as long as a message is not completely available. Completely unframed messages are forwarded as a series of `ByteBuffers`. The size of the length header must be specified (in byte) and determines the maximum frame size ($2^{8*length} - 1$ byte).

---

[5]`http://docs.oracle.com/javase/6/docs/api/java/nio/channels/ReadableByteChannel.html`, last visited: January 2012

[6]`http://docs.oracle.com/javase/6/docs/api/java/nio/channels/WritableByteChannel.html`, last visited: January 2012

AbstractHttpProxyRequestForwarder

Input : ByteBuffer
Output: ByteBuffer

The AbstractHttpProxyRequestForwarder provides a basic implementation of parsing a byte stream containing HTTP proxy requests (see 4.3.1 on page 39) by evaluating and converting HTTP proxy request headers into normal HTTP request headers, forwarding HTTP body data and establishing HTTPS tunnels, if necessary. Details about opening connections, data forwarding and dealing with HTTP syntax errors have to be implemented in application specific subclasses.

AbstractHttpProxyResponseForwarder

Input : ByteBuffer
Output: ByteBuffer

The AbstractHttpProxyResponseForwarder provides a basic implementation of parsing a byte stream containing HTTP responses (see 4.3.2 on page 48) by evaluating HTTP response headers and forwarding HTTP body data. Details about data forwarding and closing non-persistent connections have to be implemented in application specific subclasses.

SSLOutputForwarder

Input : ByteBuffer[]
Output: ByteBuffer

The SSLOutputForwarder uses javax.net.ssl.SSLEngine[7] to encrypt outbound (plaintext) data. While it encapsulates the details of the SSL handshake protocol, interested listeners can be notified about handshake protocol events. It also takes care about buffering plaintext and ciphertext as necessary. Again, interested listeners can be notified about changes in these buffer sizes.

SSLInputForwarder

Input : ByteBuffer
Output: ByteBuffer

[7] http://docs.oracle.com/javase/6/docs/api/javax/net/ssl/SSLEngine.html, last visited: January 2012

The `SSLInputForwarder` uses `SSLEngine` to decrypt inbound (ciphertext) data. It encapsulates the details of the SSL handshake protocol and also takes care about buffering plaintext and ciphertext as necessary.

More details about SSL support in the Java NIO Framework is given in section 5.6 on page 135.

5.5.2 Composite Forwarders

Composite `Forwarders` are build by combining and extending atomic `Forwarders` (see section 5.5.1 on page 126). They are used for more complex and high-level operations in the Java NIO Framework. Up to now, the following composite `Forwarders` have been implemented:

FramingOutputTransformer

`Input :` `ByteBuffer[]`
`Output:` `ByteBuffer[]`

The `FramingOutputTransformer` frames input messages by prefixing them with a header containing the length of the input message (see Figure 5.7). The `FramingOutputTransformer` computes the length header and uses an internal `PrefixTransformer` (see page 127) for the prefixing operation. The size of the length header must be specified (in byte) and determines the maximum frame size ($2^{8*length} - 1$ byte). More details about message framing with length prefixes have already been given in section 4.6.1 on page 68.

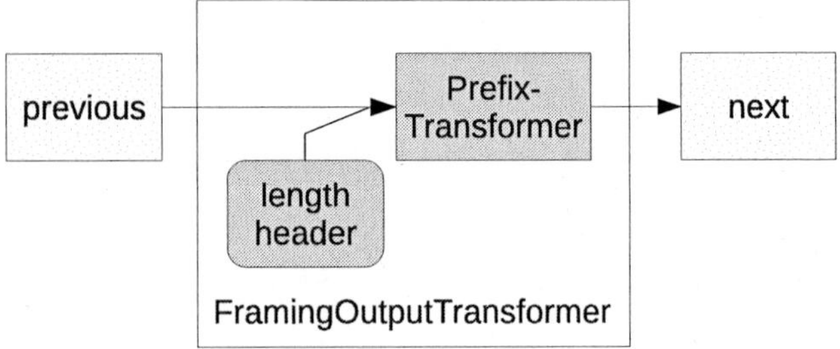

Figure 5.7: Composition of FramingOutputTransformer

DummyTrafficOutputForwarder

`Input : ByteBuffer[]`

`Output: ByteBuffer[]`

The `DummyTrafficOutputForwarder` can be used to generate dummy traffic when there is no other meaningful data available.

Enabling and disabling of dummy traffic

For many applications, generating dummy traffic is an optional and temporary feature. Therefore there must be a way to enable and disable it. There are basically two strategies to implement this:

- transformation hierarchy changes
- activation and deactivation of the dummy traffic `Forwarders`

Transformation hierarchy changes

When dummy traffic is enabled, an additional `Forwarder` (that generates dummy traffic) is integrated into the transformation hierarchy of the sender and an additional `Forwarder` (that filters dummy traffic) is integrated into the transformation hierarchy of the receiver. When dummy traffic is disabled, the additional `Forwarders` have to be removed from the transformation hierarchy.

On the positive side this strategy has less overhead (shorter transformation hierarchy, less locking, less header data) when dummy traffic is *disabled.*

On the negative side, adding and removing the `Forwarders` has to be done *at the same time*, otherwise the data stream between sender and receiver would get corrupted. This requires an out-of-bound synchronization mechanism that has to deal with many complicated details, e.g. flushing buffered data of the transformation hierarchies before changes.

Activation and Deactivation

The `Forwarders` to generate and filter dummy traffic are always present in the transformation hierarchy of an application. The `Forwarder` to generate dummy traffic can be activated (`DATA` and `DUMMY` messages are sent) and deactivated (only `DATA` messages are sent).

On the negative side this strategy has more overhead (longer transformation hierarchy, more locking, more header data) when dummy traffic is *disabled*.

On the positive side this strategy is very simple.

Because the additional overhead of an inactive dummy traffic generator is very small (one locking operation and one additional header byte) and inbound commands for synchronized transformation hierarchy changing seem to be quite complicated and error-prone, the method of activation and deactivation is used in the Java NIO Framework.

Internal design

When activated, the `DummyTrafficOutputForwarder` uses a `BufferForwarder` to store all incoming data until a data package has to be sent (see Figure 5.8).

When a data package of a certain size has to be sent, the `DummyTrafficOutputForwarder` is usually notified by a `TrafficShaperCoordinator` (which is also part of the Java NIO Framework). As the name already suggests, the `TrafficShaperCoordinator` can coordinate a collection of `TrafficShapers` (an interface of the Java NIO Framework, implemented by `DummyTrafficOutputForwarder` and other classes). The `TrafficShaperCoordinator` is using an internal `ScheduledExecutorService`[8] for periodically executing its task. The delay between task executions can be set either via a constructor parameter or via the function `setDelay(int delay)`. When executed, the `TrafficShaperCoordinator` is signaling all `TrafficShapers` in its collection that they must send a data package of a given size. The size of the data package can be set either via a constructor parameter or via the function `setPackageSize(int packageSize)`.

When the `DummyTrafficOutputForwarder` is notified by the `TrafficShaperCoordinator` to forward a data package of a certain size, it:

1. configures the `PrefixForwarder` to use a `DATA` header

2. forwards data from the `BufferForwarder` as long as there is buffered data available and the size of the data package is not reached yet

3. configures the `PrefixForwarder` to use a `DUMMY` headers

[8]`http://docs.oracle.com/javase/6/docs/api/java/util/concurrent/ScheduledExecutorService.html`, last visited: January 2012

4. creates meaningless data and forwards it to the `ByteBufferToArrayTransformer` as long as the size of the data package is not reached yet

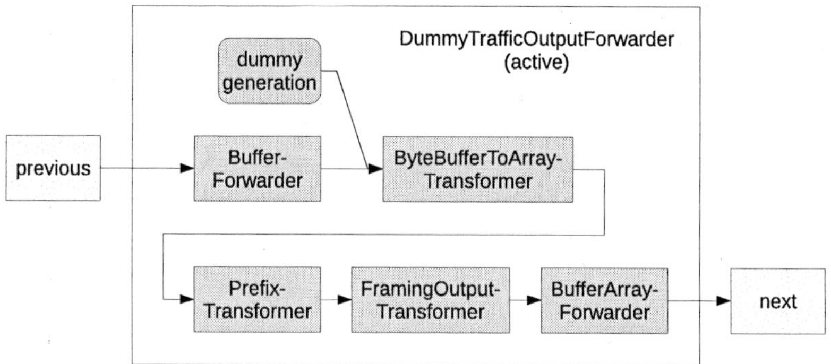

Figure 5.8: Active DummyTrafficOutputForwarder

The internal `FramingOutputTransformer` is used to frame the `DATA` and `DUMMY` messages.

After forwarding data to the next `Forwarder`, the internal `BufferArrayForwarder` might still contain framed data, because messages might become larger than the data package size (see Figure 5.9). This can happen, for example, when the message must be filled up with `DUMMY` packages but only one byte is free. Even a `DUMMY` package is at least two bytes long (one byte for the package type, one byte for the package length).

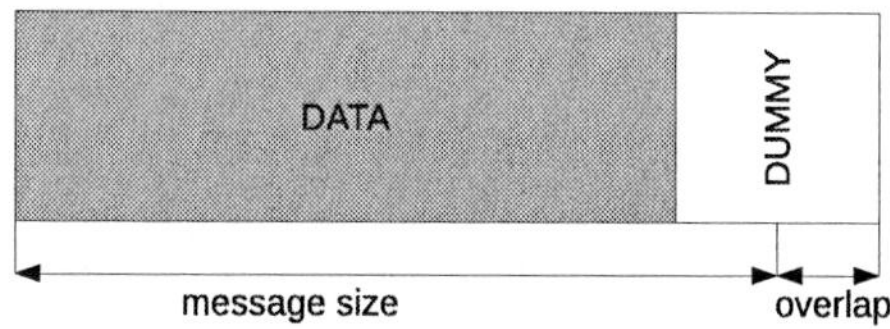

Figure 5.9: Message overlap caused by `DUMMY` message

Another reason for the internal `BufferArrayForwarder` to still contain framed

data after sending a data package is that the next `Forwarder` might not have consumed all forwarded data. Therefore, the amount of data stored in the internal `BufferArrayForwarder` must always be taken into consideration by the `DummyTrafficOutputForwarder` when sending a data package of a given size.

When deactivated, the `DummyTrafficOutputForwarder` configures the `PrefixForwarder` to use a `DATA` header and no longer uses the `BufferForwarder` to store any data but tries to forward all data directly (see Figure 5.10). Because the `FramingOutputTransformer` (see page 130) has a maximum message size, a scattering process has to be put in front, so that large input messages are divided into a series of smaller messages.

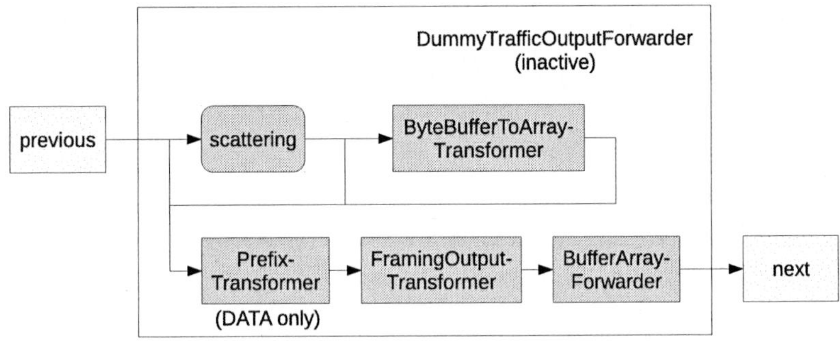

Figure 5.10: Inactive DummyTrafficOutputForwarder

DummyTrafficInputForwarder

`Input : ByteBuffer`

`Output: ByteBuffer`

The `DummyTrafficInputForwarder` removes dummy messages from a data stream and can optionally buffer data to prevent timing correlation between incoming and outgoing data packages.

It uses an internal `FramingInputForwarder` to unframe all incoming messages (see Figure 5.11). After unframing a message, the `DummyTrafficInputForwarder` checks the message type. Only the content of `DATA` messages (without the message type prefix) will be buffered or forwarded to the next forwarder, `DUMMY` messages are silently discarded. When buffering data, the `DummyTrafficInputForwarder` stores all data in a `BufferForwarder` until it gets a signal from another instance (e.g. a `TrafficShaperCoordinator`) to send a message with a certain size. An additional `ByteBufferToArrayForwarder` is necessary for type conversion between the `FramingInputForwarder` and the `BufferForwarder`.

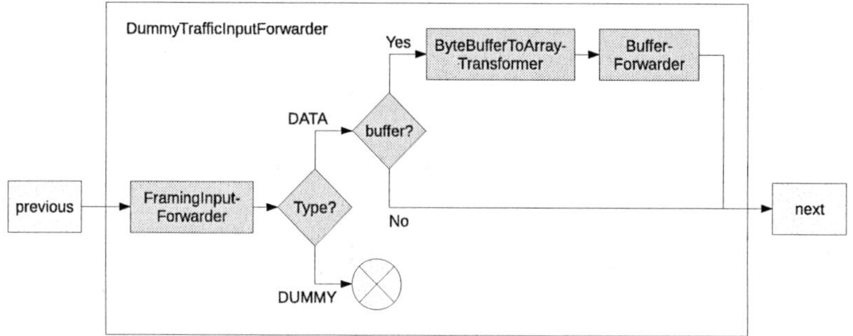

Figure 5.11: DummyTrafficInputForwarder

5.6 SSL

NIO was introduced in Java 1.4 but there was no supported way to combine it with SSL. The only supported way to establish SSL connections was to use the old blocking, stream-based classes `javax.net.ssl.SSLSocket`[9] and `SSLServerSocket`[10]. This issue was not resolved until the release of Java 5 where `SSLEngine`[11], a non-blocking and transport independent SSL implementation, was added. The `SSLEngine` provides applications with mechanisms for integrity, authentication and confidentiality and handles most details of the SSL handshake process. Data moves through the `SSLEngine` by wrapping and unwrapping Java `ByteBuffers` (see Figure 5.12).

The Java NIO Framework contains the package `ch.unifr.nio.framework.ssl` with additional helper classes, designed and implemented to make the creation of

[9] `http://docs.oracle.com/javase/6/docs/api/javax/net/ssl/SSLSocket.html`, last visited: January 2012

[10] `http://docs.oracle.com/javase/6/docs/api/javax/net/ssl/SSLServerSocket.html`, last visited: January 2012

[11] `http://docs.oracle.com/javase/6/docs/api/javax/net/ssl/SSLEngine.html`, last visited: January 2012

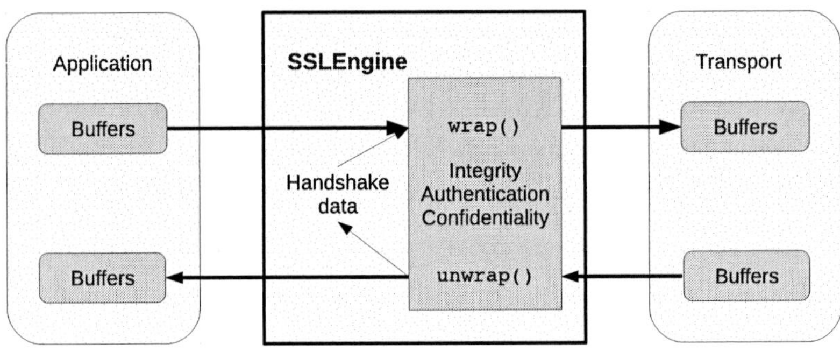

Figure 5.12: SSLEngine

applications with SSL support as easy as possible:

- `AbstractSSLChannelHandler`
  provides a base implementation for all application specific `ChannelHandlers` that need to use SSL connections. It already implements all the details when using an `SSLInputForwarder` and `SSLOutputForwarder` (see section 5.5.1 on page 129), like `SSLEngine` preparation and setting up all required cross references.

- `HandshakeCompletedListener`
  is a customized version of `HandshakeCompletedListener`[12] that works with `SSLEngine` instead of `SSLSocket`. Why such a basic interface was missing when `SSLEngine` was introduced in Java 1.5 (and is still missing in Java 6) remains unknown.

- `HandshakeNotifier`
  is a class that notifies registered (customized) `HandshakeCompletedListeners` about SSL handshake events of an `SSLEngine`.

- `SSLTools`
  is a tool class with many SSL related functions, e.g. SSL initialization and certificate checking.

[12] `http://docs.oracle.com/javase/6/docs/api/javax/net/ssl/HandshakeCompletedListener.html`, last visited: January 2012

5.7 Prevention of redundant copy operations

When using a complex hierarchy of forwarders and transformers data is buffered at different places in that hierarchy. When forwarding data through this hierarchy it happens very often that only a part of the buffered data has to be forwarded. The classical and simple approach to this problem is to create safety copies of the individual parts (see Figure 5.13). Unfortunately, this approach lowers the I/O performance of the whole hierarchy and uses unnecessary amounts of RAM.

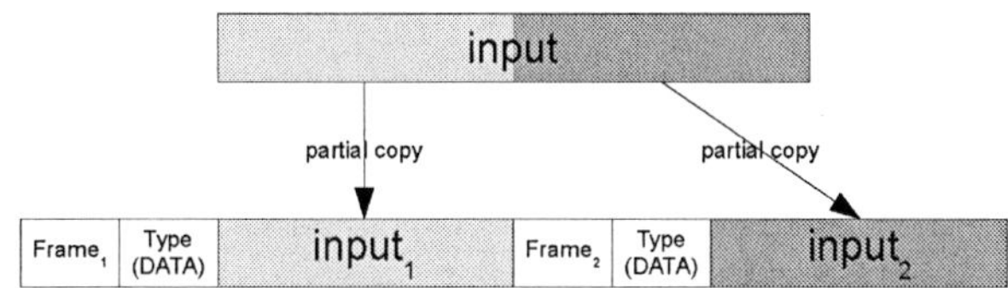

Figure 5.13: Buffer splitting with partial data copies

For storing data in its forwarders and transformers, the Java NIO Framework uses Java `ByteBuffers`. These `ByteBuffers` have an interesting feature: They can be duplicated without copying data around in memory. Instead, the content of duplicated buffers will be shared but the context information (position, limit, capacity, ...) can be set independently. By creating `ByteBuffer` duplicates and setting their positions and limits in subsequent order, data packages can be broken up into smaller parts and forwarded through a hierarchy of forwarders and transformers without creating unnecessary partial copies (see Fig 5.14).

5.8 Usage

Every application using the Java NIO Framework must start the core of the framework, the `Dispatcher`:

```
Dispatcher dispatcher = new Dispatcher();
dispatcher.start();
```

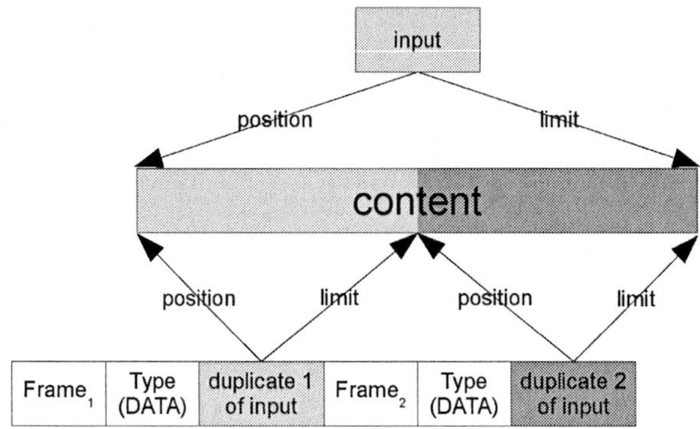

Figure 5.14: Buffer splitting with buffer duplication and content sharing

In addition to starting the `Dispatcher`, every application must also implement at least one `ChannelHandler`. The Java NIO Framework provides the abstract class `AbstractChannelHandler` that already implements the basic functionality. Instead of implementing the complete ChannelHandler interface one can just extend `AbstractChannelHandler`. For the Java NIO Framework to manage a certain channel, it must be registered at the `Dispatcher`, together with its handler:

```
dispatcher.registerChannel(channel, handler);
```

The `Dispatcher` also supports non-blocking socket connection operations. For this approach to work, the application must implement the interface `ClientSocketChannelHandler` and call:

```
dispatcher.registerClientSocketChannelHandler(
    host, port, handler);
```

This method has a variant with a timeout parameter, so that unsuccessful connection attempts can be stopped before the rather long standard TCP timeout.

All server-type applications (i.e. applications that accept socket connections) should extend the interface `AbstractAcceptor`.

Complete examples of client and server type applications using the Java NIO Framework are given online at http://nioframework.sourceforge.net/?q=node/8[13].

5.9 Conclusions

A framework for secure high-performance Java network applications that builds upon the NIO library was created. The framework combines the ease of use of classical I/O operations with the performance gain of NIO, hiding the inconvenient aspects of NIO from the developer. Developing the Java NIO framework was motivated by research on the PGA architecture, that requires high-performance network operations over secure channels. The Java NIO framework provided a tremendous performance increase, making the PGA architecture meet the requirements for anonymity servers in productive environments.

[13]last visited: January 2012

Chapter 6

Implementation

6.1 Overview

Most components of the PGA architecture are written in Java (except external components like OpenSSL in the PGA CA or some external binaries that are called in the Autostart feature of the PGA client). All graphical user interfaces have been written in Swing, using the Swing GUI Builder[1] (formerly known as Project Matisse).

6.2 Tunneling

6.2.1 I/O processing

Both the PGA Client and the PGA Server Core use a complex hierarchy of `Forwarders` for sending protocol messages, transfer application data, generate dummy traffic and provide integrity, authentication and confidentiality for the tunnel between them (see Figure 6.1).

For receiving data from the tunnel both the PGA Client and the PGA Server Core use the chain of `Forwarders` shown in Figure 6.2:

- The `ChannelReader` is used to read the data stream from the tunnel.
- The `SSLInputForwarder` is used for SSL handshaking, authentication and decrypting the received data.

[1] **`http://netbeans.org/features/java/swing.html`**, last visited: January 2012

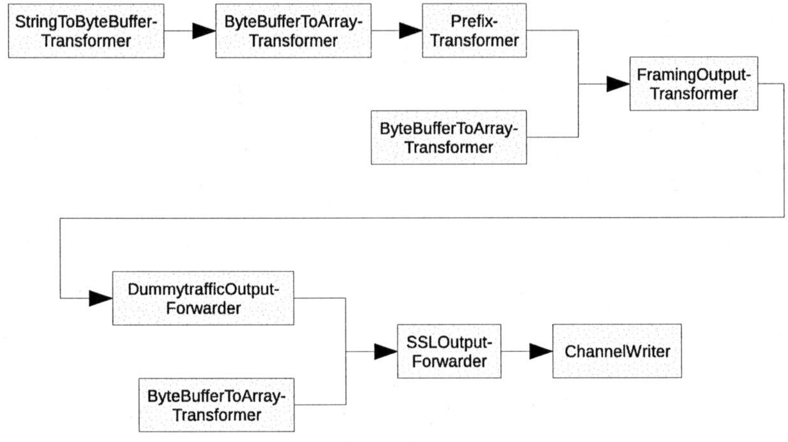

Figure 6.1: PGA tunnel sending hierarchy

- The `DummyTrafficInputForwarder` is used to filter `DUMMY` messages and forward `DATA` messages.
- The `FramingInputTransformer` is used to unframe the received message frames.
- The `PgaClientForwarder`/`PgaServerForwarder` is not part of the Java NIO Framework but an application specific `Forwarder` of the PGA Client or PGA Server Core that processes all received messages according to their type.

Figure 6.2: PGA tunnel receiving hierarchy

6.2.2 Dummy traffic coordination

On the PGA Client side, only one `TrafficShaperCoordinator` is needed and it must only handle one `TrafficShaper`, the `DummyTrafficOutputForwarder` of the tunnel to the PGA Server Core. In contrast to that, one `TrafficShaperCoordinator` is needed for every established anonymity group on the PGA Server Core side (see Figure 6.3).

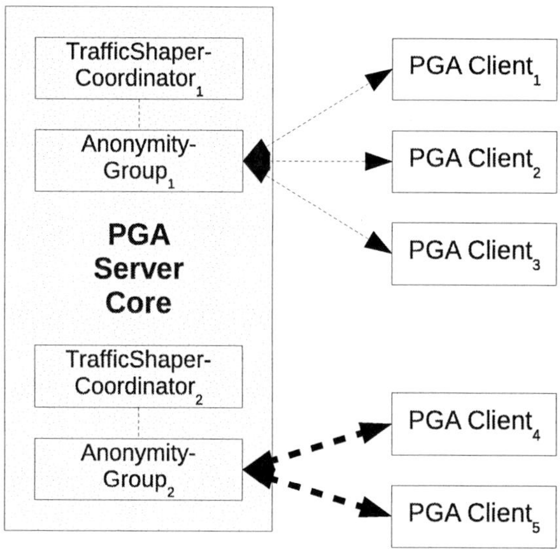

Figure 6.3: PGA Server Core dummy traffic coordination

6.2.3 Message representation

Most tunneling protocol messages only consist of simple information (target address, ...). But some messages contain a lot of detailed, structured information, e.g. the `DYNAMIC_STATE` message (see 4.6.2 on page 70). For these types of messages, the Java objects containing the necessary information are converted to an XML representation with the help of the JavaBeans `XMLEncoder`[2].

The JavaBeans `XMLDecoder`[3] is used for parsing the XML representations back to Java objects. One advantage of using the JavaBeans `XMLEncoder` and `XMLDecoder`

[2] `http://docs.oracle.com/javase/6/docs/api/java/beans/XMLEncoder.html`, last visited: January 2012

[3] `http://docs.oracle.com/javase/6/docs/api/java/beans/XMLDecoder.html`, last visited: January 2012

is that the XML representation is not bound to the Java Virtual Machine (as it would have been when using the binary object representations created by `ObjectOutputStream`[4] and parsed by `ObjectInputStream`[5]) but can easily be created and parsed by other implementations in different programming languages.

6.2.4 Protection against bandwidth attacks

If the negotiated encryption mechanisms are visible in the SSL handshake, then it may well be that the characteristics of the mechanism (e.g. block size) are also known. This way it may be possible to guess the clear text bandwidth by observing the cipher text bandwidth. It may happen that different members of an anonymity group use different SSL parameters (asymmetric cipher, symmetric cipher and hash function). If all members of this anonymity group would use the same cipher text bandwidth it could happen that, because of the different SSL parameters, that they actually use different clear text bandwidths because some parameters generate more overhead than others. This would divide the anonymity group as shown in the following example:

There are two groups of members in an anonymity group. The first group uses SSL parameters that result in a plain text bandwidth b_{p1}, the second group uses SSL parameters that result in a plain text bandwidth b_{p2}.The bandwidths are different so that $b_{p1} < b_{p2}$. The common cipher text bandwidth of the anonymity group is b_c (see Figure 6.4).

If an adversary observes a plain text data stream at the PGA Server Core with the bandwidth b_{p2} it is immediately clear that this data stream must originate from a member of the second group. (If an adversary observes a plain text data stream with the bandwidth b_{p1}, no conclusion can be made because the data stream could originate from any member of the anonymity group. It is always possible to *not* use the full available plain text bandwidth.)

To prevent this kind of attack, all members of an anonymity group must use the same maximum *plain text* bandwidth (see Figure 6.5). An attacker can not use the different cipher text bandwidths to execute the attack described above.

---

[4]`http://docs.oracle.com/javase/6/docs/api/java/io/ObjectOutputStream.html`, last visited: January 2012

[5]`http://docs.oracle.com/javase/6/docs/api/java/io/ObjectInputStream.html`, last visited: January 2012

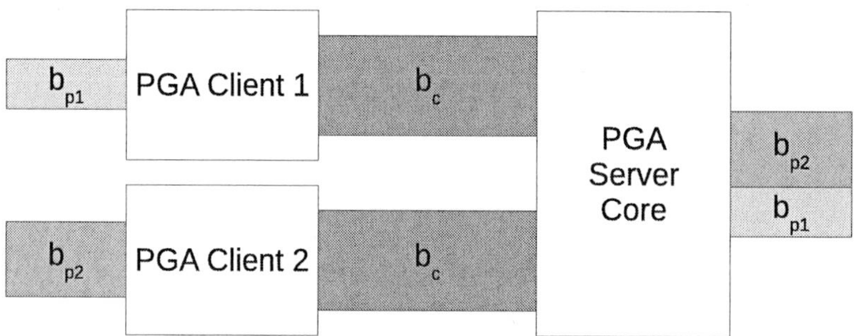

Figure 6.4: Plaintext bandwidth attack

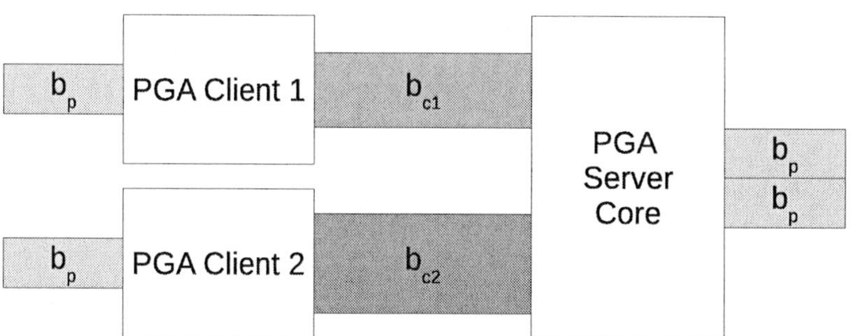

Figure 6.5: Plaintext bandwidth attack prevented

6.3 Target I/O handling

Both the PGA Client and the PGA Server Core read from and write data to connection targets. At the PGA Client side these connection targets are usually local applications, at the PGA Server Core side they are usually web servers. Both PGA Client and PGA Server Core use application specific Java NIO Framework `ChannelHandlers` to implement this functionality (see Figure 6.6).

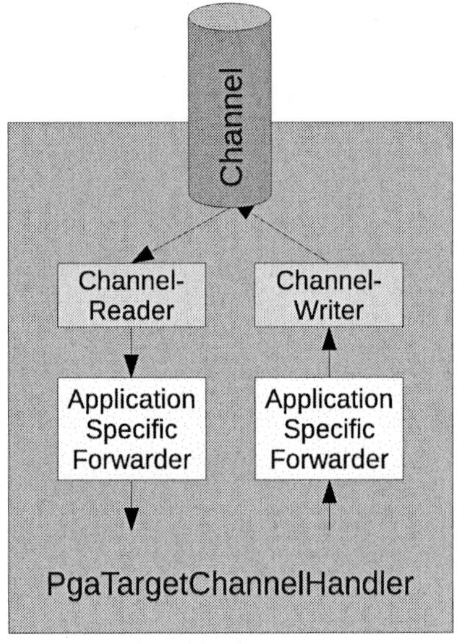

Figure 6.6: PGA target handling

The class hierarchy of Java NIO Framework `ChannelHandlers` used in PGA for target I/O handling is shown in Figure 6.7.

The abstract class `PgaTargetChannelHandler` implements the `XON/XOFF` flow control (see section 4.6.4 on page 88) and handling of buffer size changes.

The class `PgaServerTargetChannelHandler` implements the state machine for PGA Server Core target connections shown in Figure 4.13 on page 82, executes the target I/O operations and implements the necessary error handling.

The abstract class `PgaClientTargetChannelHandler` implements the state ma-

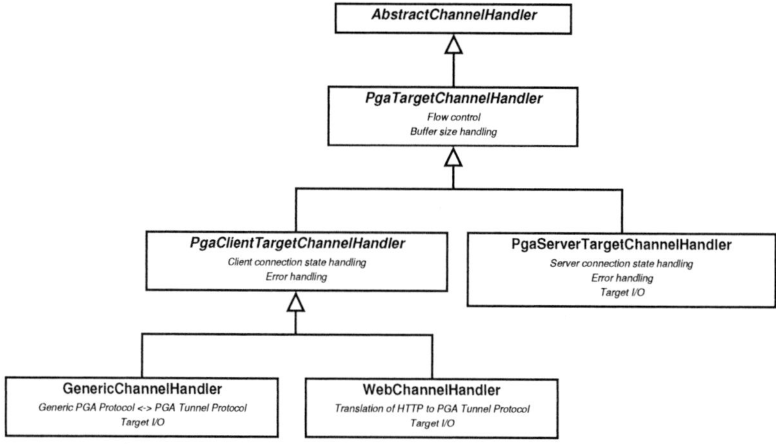

Figure 6.7: Class hierarchy of PGA target channel handlers

chine for PGA Client target connections shown in Figure 4.11 on page 80 and implements the necessary error handling.

The class `GenericChannelHandler` implements the protocol translation between the generic PGA application protocol (see section 4.2.2 on 35) and the PGA Tunnel protocol (see section 4.6 on page 67).

The class `WebChannelHandler` implements the protocol translation between HTTP and the PGA Tunnel protocol. For this task it uses internally the Java NIO Framework `Forwarders` `AbstractHttpProxyRequestForwarder` and `AbstractHttpProxy-ResponseForwarder` (see section 5.5.1 on page 129).

6.4 Server

The PGA Server Core is implemented in Java, using the Java NIO Framework (see chapter 5 on page 107 for details) for secure and scalable I/O operations.

6.4.1 Address resolution

When the Java NIO Framework `Dispatcher` thread runs, it executes the `Handler-Adapters` of all `Channels` via an `Executor`. This way, serving the `Channels` can be done in parallel and be scalable. In contrast to this, reading, parsing, buffering and forwarding the data of a single `Channel` through its transformation chain is done by one single execution thread. This results in the following implementation details:

The PGA Server Core creates application independent TCP connections by first parsing the address information of an `OPEN` message in a Java NIO Framework execution thread. Most of the time, the address information is unresolved, i.e. it consists of an unresolved host name instead of a resolved IP address and a port number. Resolving a host name to its IP address is a blocking operation that can take a very long time. When the host name would be resolved in the execution thread itself, the PGA Server would stop processing the next messages of the regarding PGA Client, which severely degrades the performance of the anonymous connection as shown by the following example:

1. The PGA Client sends two `OPEN` messages in a row, one to `serverA:80` and the next one to `serverB:8080`.

2. The PGA Server Core parses the first `OPEN` message and blocks a long time while trying to determine the IP address for the host name `serverA`.

3. The connection to `serverB` does not get established until the IP address of `serverA` is finally resolved (or failed to resolve).

To avoid this scenario, the PGA Server Core stops processing an `OPEN` message in the Java NIO Framework execution thread after extracting the address information and passes the host name, port, pending connection ID, initial connection data and the currently used `ChannelHandler` to an `Executor`. The worker thread of this `Executor` is resolving (or failing to resolve) the host name and (if resolving was successful) continuing with opening the target connection and buffering and forwarding the initial connection data.

6.4.2 CPU load detection

The CPU load of the PGA Server Core gets transmitted in `DynamicServerState` messages from the PGA Server Core to the PGA Client and is presented in the graphical user interface of the PGA Client (see 4.2.1 on page 31).

Until now, this information is only available when the PGA Server Core is running on a Linux operating system. The PGA Server Core parses the information that is available in the Linux Kernel statistics file /proc/stat. Details about the syntax and semantic of this file are described in the Linux Kernel documentation[6].

CPU load detection for other operating systems (where this information is not available in easily accessible files) can be added by using the Java Native Interface[7].

6.4.3 Remote file browsing

When selecting key stores and certificates on the PGA Server Core machine via the PGA Remote Management, the user must be able to browse the file system of the PGA Server Core machine. This was implemented with the Java Management Extension.

On the PGA Server Core side, the interface JMXFileSystemViewMBean was created. It specifies all methods that are necessary for browsing files with a standard Swing file chooser. This interface was implemented by the class JMXFileSystemView.

On the PGA Remote Management side, the class JMXFsView that extends javax.swing.filechooser.FileSystemView and calls JMXFileSystemViewMBean for all file chooser operations was implemented. Because the standard Swing file chooser works with the class java.io.File, the additional class JMXFile that extends java.io.File and also calls JMXFileSystemViewMBean for all file chooser operations was implemented.

When selecting key stores and certificates from the graphical user interface of the PGA Remote Management, the Swing file chooser is created with the file system viewer JMXFsView. This way, all file chooser operations are executed via Java Management Extension on the PGA Server Core.

6.4.4 Anonymity group management

For simplicity reasons, the PGA Server Core currently only implements server defined anonymity groups (see 4.4.1 on page 59). User defined anonymity groups can be implemented by future works.

[6] http://kernel.org/doc/Documentation/filesystems/proc.txt, last visited: January 2012

[7] http://docs.oracle.com/javase/6/docs/technotes/guides/jni/index.html, last visited: January 2012

6.4.5 User management

The ChannelReaders and ChannelWriters of the Java NIO Framework provide an interface for PropertyChangeListeners. They are notified whenever data is read or written. This interface is used on the PGA Server Core side for accounting the traffic created and consumed by anonymous users.

A simple token bucket algorithm is used for shaping the bandwidth for anonymous users.

Due to time constraints a complete user management was not implemented in the PGA Server Core. This can be completed by future works. For simplicity reasons it is recommended to use a database that provides an embedded JDBC driver, e.g. Apache Derby[8].

6.4.6 Traffic accounting

When sending and receiving data via the PGA architecture, different types of data is used, generated, forwarded and filtered out. When sending, there can be two different data sources:

Data
: the real payload data from applications that use the PGA architecture

Protocol
: PGA protocol overhead, e.g. state update requests or responses.

All Forwarders of the message sending I/O hierarchy (see Figure 6.8) generate some types of data:

- The PrefixTransformer generates protocol information (e.g. the message type or connection ID).
- The FramingOutputTransformer generates protocol information (the framing length header).
- The DummyTrafficOutputForwarder generates protocol information (the internal type prefix and framing length header) and dummy traffic.

[8] http://db.apache.org/derby/, last visited: January 2012

- The SSLOutputForwarder generates communications overhead because of SSL (handshake data, SSL protocol information, cipher block padding, ...).

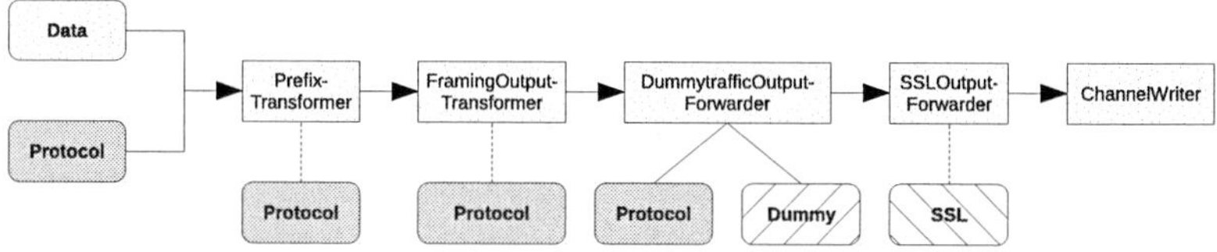

Figure 6.8: Message sending data types

PGA users and administrators should be able to check the functioning of the Forwarders of the PGA tunnel I/O hierarchy. A simple and effective instrument is to provide a visual feedback in terms of a bandwidth-time graph for all different types of data.

The I/O hierarchy of the PGA architecture is very complex and contains many components that buffer data or generate additional data. Therefore the question arises, where in the architecture the different types of data should be measured and shown to the user so that they show a coherent picture of the inner workings of the I/O hierarchy.

When measuring the different data types at the entry point of the I/O transformation hierarchy, it is easy to differentiate between payload data and protocol data but the more interesting operations (dummy traffic and encryption) would be left out. Another interesting measuring point would be where the user has the adversary's view. Because the goal of the PGA architecture is to protect against an adversary in the network, this would be the exiting point of the ChannelWriter. Unfortunately, at this point in the architecture, only encrypted data is visible. There is another interesting measuring point: the transition from the DummyTrafficOutputForwarder to the SSLOutputForwarder. At this point it is still possible to differentiate between data and dummy traffic. Because buffering data in the SSLOutputForwarder and the ChannelWriter only happens in very rare situations, it is possible to measure at the same time the bandwidth of the SSL traffic and still have a coherent picture of the overall situation of the different data type bandwidths at this point in the architecture. Unfortunately, it is not possible any more at this measuring point to differentiate between payload data and protocol data because they have been merged in the BufferForwarder of the DummyTrafficOutputForwarder (see section 5.5.2 on page 131 for more details).

Because there is no measuring point in the architecture that gives a complete and coherent picture of all different data types, bandwidth measuring is done by introducing atomic counters[9] at *every* Forwarder in the I/O hierarchy. Atomic counters are single variables that support thread-safe but lock-free updating and reading, i.e. they can be accessed in a multi-threaded architecture, as the Java NIO Framework provides, without the need for additional synchronization mechanisms and therefore have a much better performance than classical counting mechanisms.

In summary, the current approach of measuring all data types on every Forwarder all the time can only represent an approximation of the real situation.

6.4.7 Misuse discouragement

The PGA Server can be configured to monitor connection attempts and produce logging files. This feature can only be activated by PGA Server administrators. Filtering rules can be expressed with regular expressions. There are two types of rules:

Domain rules: In the domain rules the administrator can specify patterns for connection attempts to certain domains. The rules have to be specified with the following pattern:

<source IP> → <destination domain:port>

IP rules: In the IP rules the administrator can specify patterns for connection attempts to certain IP addresses. The rules have to be specified with the following pattern:

<source IP> → <destination IP:port>

It is necessary to have both domain and IP rules because of the dynamic nature of DNS. A web server with a single IP could be accessed via many different host names, on the other hand side a host name can by dynamically resolved to many different IP addresses.

[9] http://docs.oracle.com/javase/6/docs/api/java/util/concurrent/atomic/AtomicLong.html, last visited: January 2012

All rules are processed with the logical *OR* operation, i.e. if any rule matches the current connection attempt, the matching operation stops and the connection attempt is recorded.

In the PGA architecture the PGA Server Core must resolve the destination host names given by any PGA Clients to their IP address. Therefore the information needed for the filter rules above is always present. In the PGA architecture it is nowhere necessary to get the host names of the source IP addresses. The PGA anonymity service works even when the IP address of a machine running the PGA Client can not be mapped to a host name (called "reverse name lookup"). Because the PGA server never needs to execute a reverse name lookup, it is impossible to specify source domains in the filtering rules. If the need arises in the future to express filtering rules based on source domains, it should be noted that this process slows down the misuse discouragement architecture because log entries can not be written instantly but need to wait until the reverse name lookup finishes. Reverse name lookup can be arbitrary long before it succeeds or runs into a timeout. So that all the log entries are still in order when written to disk or into a database, a FIFO logging queue would be necessary where all the log records are inserted into the tail and only entries where the reverse name lookup finished are removed from the head of the queue and written to a persistent data storage.

The connection attempts are recorded into a set of rotating log files that are compressed and encrypted with a given public GPG[10] key when the log files rotate. This mechanism is very simple but leaves a short window of vulnerability (the last log file is always open for writing, uncompressed and unencrypted).

Users of the PGA anonymity architecture are informed if a PGA Server Core monitors connections or not via the dynamic server status update information that is presented in the PGA Client (see section 4.2.1 on page 31).

6.4.8 Testing

While implementing the target connection state machines for both the PGA Client and the PGA Server Core, several mechanisms for unit testing, integration testing and system testing have been applied. The current implementation uses the testing

[10]GNU Privacy Guard, see `http://gnupg.org`, last visited: January 2012

frameworks JUnit[11] and Jemmy[12].

For integration testing a complete PGA scenario (with client applications and web servers) is needed. Therefore some dummy programs have been written to simulate the peripheral software components (see Figure 6.9).

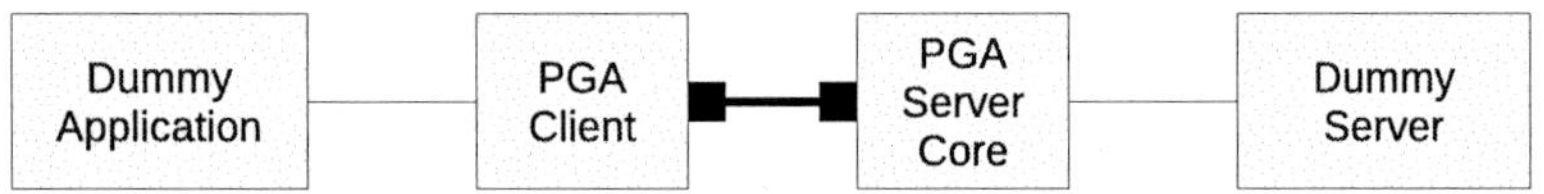

Figure 6.9: Integration testing scenario for the PGA tunnel state machine

For simple functional tests, the dummy application must send some random data. This data must then be intercepted at the dummy server side and checked that every byte sent at the dummy application was also received by the dummy server.

The connection shutdown procedures can be tested by first establishing a data connection and then shutting down the sockets of the dummy components. After some time-out it must be verified if the expected changes took place on the respective peer side socket.

In addition to checking the peripheral dummy components the internal state changes of the PGA components (e.g. clearing of the target register index) must be also verified. If the PGA components are written in object oriented style the state holding items are most probably hidden by information hiding and encapsulation measures. One solution would be to break up the encapsulation and provide access methods to internal states just for the purpose of testing. For the current PGA implementation this was unnecessary because it is written in Java and the Java platform provides a reflection mechanism [20] that enables access to encapsulated fields while running tests. This way the strong encapsulation of the PGA components does not have to be softened.

One part of the error handling of the PGA state machines can be verified by just closing the socket of a dummy component while data is transferred.

The part that handles unplugged network cables or crashed operation systems is exceptionally more difficult to test. It is not enough to terminate the dummy applications. The "problem" is that today's operating systems always correctly close

[11] `http://www.junit.org`, last visited: January 2012

[12] `http://jemmy.java.net/`, last visited: January 2012

the sockets of terminated applications. Therefore it is probably impossible to run such tests with all components on one single machine. The solution that is used for the current implementation is to use several virtual machines that are terminated during the tests. The generic and open source machine emulator and virtualizer QEMU[13] was used for these tests (see Figure 6.10).

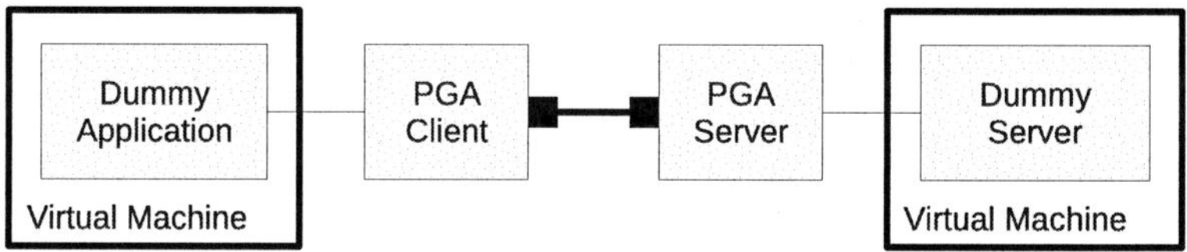

Figure 6.10: Advanced integration testing scenario for the PGA tunnel state machine

Both virtual machines are almost identical. The only difference is the application that automatically starts at the end of the operation system boot sequence. To minimize the efforts for maintaining the virtual machines only one machine should be effectively maintained and the other one should be a clone of the first. Every time the machine is cloned (e.g. after updating the dummy components or other significant changes) only the start-up sequence of the clone has to be modified. In QEMU, a clone of a virtual machine is created with the following command (if the original machine is called "original.img" and the clone should be called "clone.img"):

```
qemu-img create -b original.img -f qcow2 clone.img
```

Both virtual machines can be started in parallel and virtually crashed (or "virtually switched off") when running the tests. To protect the file system of both virtual machines, they should be started in a so-called "snapshot mode", i.e. changes to the file system are volatile - the file system in the guest operating systems during the tests can not be damaged.

6.5 Remote Management

The first implementation of the PGA Remote Management was a standalone Swing based application using a simple custom protocol. This version was canceled after the emergence of the standard Java Management Extension.

[13] `http://wiki.qemu.org`, last visited: January 2012

The second implementation was based on JConsole[14]. JConsole provides a plug-in API that defines the `com.sun.tools.jconsole.JConsolePlugin` abstract class that can be extended to build a custom plug-in. After working on a PGA Remote Management plug-in for JConsole, I noticed some shortcomings of JConsole and (as JConsole is an Open Source project) fixed these shortcomings and provided the patches to the JConsole developers. The response was very positive but at the same time I was notified that JConsole was expired and would be replaced by Java VisualVM[15], a solution based on the integrated development environment and application platform NetBeans[16].

The statistics graphs of the PGA Remote Management are implemented with the help of JRobin[17], a Java port of RRDTool[18], a data logging and graphing system for time series data.

A basic HTML adaptor for JMX is provided in the JMX Reference implementation[19]. The library `jmxtools.jar` provides the class `com.sun.jdmk.comm.HtmlAdaptorServer` that can be registered at a standard MBeans server. The API of `HtmlAdaptorServer` provides the function `setPort(int port)` which can be used to specify the port of the adaptors integrated webserver. This way it is possible to remotely manage the PGA Server Core from a simple web browser as shown in figure 6.11 where the management front end is a small screen Nokia N900[20] smartphone.

6.6 Client

6.6.1 Autostart

The autostart feature depends on the login procedure of every supported desktop environment on every supported operating system. In addition to that, starting

[14] `http://docs.oracle.com/javase/6/docs/technotes/guides/management/jconsole.html`, last visited: January 2012

[15] `http://visualvm.java.net`, last visited: January 2012

[16] `http://netbeans.org`, last visited: January 2012

[17] `http://sourceforge.net/projects/jrobin/`, last visited: January 2012

[18] `http://oss.oetiker.ch/rrdtool/`, last visited: January 2012

[19] `http://www.oracle.com/technetwork/java/javase/tech/download-jsp-141676.html`, last visited: January 2012

[20] `http://en.wikipedia.org/wiki/Nokia_N900`, last visited: January 2012

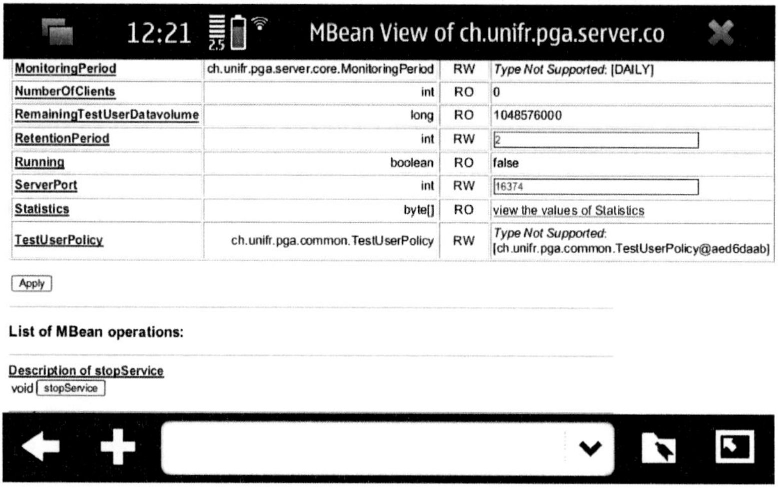

Figure 6.11: Remote Management via HTML Adaptor

up the PGA Client depends on how it was started (executable JAR file, Java Web Start, application bundle, ...). Because of the complexity and usefulness of the autostart feature, a generic, re-usable tool class `ch.unifr.pga.tools.AutoStarter` was implemented.

The constructor of `ch.unifr.pga.tools.AutoStarter` is implemented as

```
AutoStarter(String jnlpFileName, String osxDockName,
            String osxScriptsDirName, String osxLaunchAgentsFileName,
            String options)
```

`jnlpFileName` is the name of the Java Network Launching Protocol[21] file

`osxDockName` is the name of the application in the Mac OS X dock

`osxScriptsDirName` is the name of the Mac OS X directory for application specific scripts

`osxLaunchAgentsFileName` is the name of the Mac OS X launch agents file

[21] `http://docs.oracle.com/javase/6/docs/technotes/guides/javaws/developersguide/syntax.html`, last visited: January 2012

options are the optional application command line options (not the command line options for the Java Virtual Machine)

Startup command

When the application was started via Java Web Start, the corresponding command is:

```
javaws [-open <command line options>] <JNLP URL>
```

command line options is the placeholder for the optional application command line options

JNLP URL is the placeholder for the mandatory JNLP URL (with the syntax <JNLP codebase>/<jnlpFileName>.jnlp)

When the application was started by running its executable JAR file, the corresponding command differs for every supported desktop environment. On Linux, the command is:

```
java -jar <JAR file path> [command line options]
```

where <JAR file path> is the placeholder for the mandatory path to the applications executable JAR file.

On Mac OS X it is possible to create a Mac OS X application bundle from an executable JAR file, e.g. with JarBundler[22]. When the application was started by running its executable JAR file, the command is:

```
java [-Xdock:name=<name>] -jar <JAR file path> [command line options]
```

where name is the placeholder for the optional name of the application in the Mac OS X dock. When the application was started from an application bundle, the command is:

```
exec <JAR file path>/.app/Contents/MacOS/JavaApplicationStub
     [command line options]
```

[22] http://www.informagen.com/JarBundler/, last visited: January 2012

Autostart configuration

The means to automatically start a command when logging in differs for every desktop environment. The API of `ch.unifr.pga.tools.AutoStarter` provides the following methods to enable or disable the autostart feature on all supported operating systems:

```
enableAutoStart(String windowsRunTreeKey,
            String linuxIconSource, String linuxIconFileName,
            String linuxDesktopFileTemplate, String linuxDesktopFileName)

disableAutoStart(String windowsRunTreeKey,
            String linuxIconFileName, String linuxDesktopFileName)
```

Linux

To enable the autostart feature on Linux, the last four parameters of `enableAutoStart()` are used:

`linuxIconSource` is the String to specify the location of the application icon with the method `Class.getResourceAsStream(String name)`. This way the application icon can be contained in the executable JAR file.

`linuxIconFileName` is the path of the file where to store the application icon. For the PGA Client, the following path is used:
`~/.java/.userPrefs/ch/unifr/pga/client/PgaClient/pga_client.png`

`linuxDesktopFileTemplate` is a template for a file following the freedesktop.org[23] Desktop Entry Specification[24]. The template for the PGA Client is:

```
[Desktop Entry]
Type=Application
Name=PGA Client
Name[de]=PGA-Client
Icon={0}
Exec={1}
```

[23] `http://www.freedesktop.org`, last visited: January 2012

[24] `http://standards.freedesktop.org/desktop-entry-spec/latest/`, last visited: January 2012

`linuxDesktopFileName` is the base name of the desktop file to create (without the `.desktop` suffix)

Enabling autostart on Linux works in three steps:

1. the icon is copied to the specified destination file
2. the desktop file template is filled (`{0}` is replaced by the path to the application icon and `{1}` is replaced by the necessary startup command, depending on how the PGA Client was started
3. following the freedesktop.org Desktop Application Autostart Specification[25] the filled desktop file is copied into the standard autostart directory `~/.config/autostart/<linuxDesktopFileName>.desktop`.

To disable the autostart feature on Linux, the last two parameters of `disableAutoStart()` are used to remove both the icon and the desktop file previously produced by the function `enableAutoStart()`.

Mac OS X

To enable the autostart feature on Mac OS X, the variables provided in the `AutoStarter` constructor are used:

1. A simple shell script `~/Library/Scripts/Applications/<osxScriptsDirName>/autostart.sh` with the content

   ```
   #!/bin/sh
   <startup command>
   ```

   is created and made executable.

[25] `http://standards.freedesktop.org/autostart-spec/autostart-spec-latest.html`, last visited: January 2012

2. The property list file[26]
   `~/Library/LaunchAgents/<osxLaunchAgentsFileName>.plist`
   is created with the following content:

```
<?xml version="1.0" encoding="UTF-8"?>
<!DOCTYPE plist PUBLIC "-//Apple Computer//DTD PLIST 1.0//EN"
  "http://www.apple.com/DTDs/PropertyList-1.0.dtd">
<plist version="1.0">
<dict>
  <key>Label</key>
  <string>autostart</string>
  <key>ProgramArguments</key>
  <array>
    <string><scriptFile></string>
  </array>
  <key>RunAtLoad</key>
  <true/>
</dict>
</plist>
```

   where `<scriptFile>` is replaced with the path to the simple shell script created in step (1).

To disable the autostart feature on Mac OS X, the directory `~/Library/Scripts/Applications/<osxScriptsDirName>` and the file `~/Library/LaunchAgents/<osxLaunchAgentsFileName>.plist` are removed.

Windows

To enable the autostart feature on Windows, the parameter `windowsRunTreeKey` of `enableAutoStart()` is used to add the startup command to the Windows registry node `HKEY_CURRENT_USER\Software\Microsoft\Windows\CurrentVersion\Run`

Adding an entry to the Windows registry is done by

[26] `http://developer.apple.com/library/mac/#documentation/Darwin/Reference/ManPages/man5/plist.5.html`, last visited: January 2012

1. creating a temporary, UTF-16 encoded file with the content:

```
Windows Registry Editor Version 5.00

[<node>]
"<key>"=<value>
```

2. executing the command:

```
cmd.exe /c regedit /s <path of temporary file>
```

To disable the autostart feature on Windows, the `windowsRunTreeKey` is removed from the Windows registry.

Removing an entry from the Windows registry is done by

1. creating a temporary, UTF-16 encoded file with the content:

```
Windows Registry Editor Version 5.00

[<node>]
"<key>"=-
```

2. executing the command:

```
cmd.exe /c regedit /s <path of temporary file>
```

6.6.2 Automatic Proxy reconfiguration

The goal of automatic proxy reconfiguration is to reconfigure common applications automatically so that these applications communicate via the PGA Client when it starts and without the PGA Client when it quits. At the time of this writing the only application fully supported by the PGA Client is web browsing. Therefore, the focus of the implementation of this feature was to automatically reconfigure common web browsers on several supported operating systems.

Firefox

Firefox[27] is a free web browser by the Mozilla Corporation[28]. It is available for a wide range of operating systems. The automatic proxy reconfiguration for Firefox was implemented for Linux and Windows.

Linux

Reconfiguring Firefox on Linux is done by changing the Firefox configuration file `~/.mozilla/firefox/*/prefs.js`.

Before changing the Firefox configuration file, the PGA Client checks if there is an instance of Firefox already running. This is done by running the command

```
ps -U <userName>
```

where `<userName>` is a placeholder for the mandatory name of the current user, and checking the output for processes named `firefox-bin`. When running instances of Firefox are found, the user is presented a message asking if the PGA Client may restart Firefox. If the user agreed to restart Firefox, all of its instances are quit with the command

```
killall -9 firefox-bin
```

If no instance of Firefox is running, the Firefox configuration file is changed.

When starting the PGA Client, the original configuration file values are saved for later use and the following changes are made:

- `network.proxy.type` is set to `1`, the value for manual proxy configuration.
- `network.proxy.http` and `network.proxy.ssl` are set to `"localhost"` because this is where the PGA Client Web Connector is running.
- `network.proxy.http_port` and `network.proxy.ssl_port` are set to the service port of the PGA Client Web Connector.

When stopping the PGA Client, the original configuration file values are restored in the configuration file.

[27] `http://www.firefox.com`, last visited: January 2012
[28] `http://www.mozilla.com`, last visited: January 2012

Windows

On Windows, the destination of the Firefox configuration file must be queried from the Windows registry. The key `AppData` in the registry tree `HKEY_CURRENT_USER\Software\Microsoft\Windows\CurrentVersion\Explorer\Shell Folders` contains the path to the application data directory of the current user. Within this directory, the Firefox configuration file is found in `Mozilla\Firefox\Profiles\*\prefs.js`

Changes to the Firefox configuration file are done the same way as on Linux.

Checking, if an instance of Firefox is running, is done on Windows by running the command `tasklist` and checking the output for a process named `firefox.exe`.

Quitting all running instances of Firefox on Windows is done via the command

```
taskkill /F /IM firefox.exe
```

where `/F` is the command switch to force quitting the application and `/IM` is the command switch where to specify the image name of the process to quit (`firefox.exe` in this case).

KDE

KDE[29] is a graphical desktop for several operating systems, including Linux and Windows. It supports central proxy configuration. Reconfiguring the KDE proxy configuration is done by changing the KIO[30] configuration file `~/.kde/share/config/kioslaverc`.

When starting the PGA Client, the original configuration file values are saved for later use and the following changes are made:

- `ProxyType` is set to `1`, the value for manual proxy configuration.
- `httpProxy` and `httpsProxy` are set to `http://localhost:<port>`, where `<port>` is the placeholder for the mandatory service port of the PGA Client Web Connector.

KDE applications do not have to be restarted to reparse their proxy configuration. The proxy configuration in KDE 3 can be changed on-the-fly via DCOP[31] by

[29] `http://www.kde.org`, last visited: January 2012

[30] `http://en.wikipedia.org/wiki/KIO`, last visited: January 2012

[31] Desktop COmmunications Protocol, see `http://techbase.kde.org/Development/Architecture/DCOP`, last visited: January 2012

executing the command

```
dcop <program> KIO::Scheduler reparseSlaveConfiguration http
```

where <program> is the placeholder for the mandatory name of the program that should reparse its I/O slave HTTP configuration. Unfortunately, the mandatory <program> parameter made it necessary to maintain a list of known KDE applications. Whenever the proxy configuration should be automatically changed, every application in this list had to be checked, if it was currently running and only then the dcop call would be executed. This was very complex and error-prone.

In KDE 4, DCOP was deprecated and replaced by DBUS[32]. The proxy configuration in KDE 4 can be changed on-the-fly by executing the command

```
dbus-send --type=signal /KIO/Scheduler \
   org.kde.KIO.Scheduler.reparseSlaveConfiguration string:""
```

This is much simpler than in KDE 3 because the proxy configuration of *all* KDE programs is automatically changed and no application list has to be maintained.

When stopping the PGA Client, the original configuration file values are restored in the configuration file.

Internet Explorer

The Internet Explorer[33] is a web browser that is only available for Microsoft Windows operating systems.

Reconfiguring the proxy settings of Internet Explorer is done by changing the registry tree
HKEY_CURRENT_USER\Software\Microsoft\Windows\CurrentVersion\Internet Settings.

When starting the PGA Client, the original registry key values are saved for later use and the following changes are made:

- the key ProxyEnable is set to dword:00000001
- the key ProxyServer is set to "http=localhost:<port>;https=localhost:<port>", where <port> is the placeholder for the mandatory service port of the PGA Client Web Connector.

[32]http://www.freedesktop.org/wiki/Software/dbus, last visited: January 2012

[33]http://windows.microsoft.com/en-US/internet-explorer/products/ie/home, last visited: January 2012

Identically to Firefox, Internet Explorer also needs to be restarted after applying the changes to the proxy settings.

When stopping the PGA Client, the original proxy configuration values are restored in the Windows registry.

6.6.3 Bandwidth charts

The bandwidth charts in the PGA Client are implemented using the free chart library JFreeChart[34].

6.7 Certificate Authority

The core functions of the PGA Certificate Authority use OpenSSL [65] to create private keys and certificates.

A graphical user interface for the PGA CA was implemented in Java, using the Swing toolkit. The graphical user interface is used for providing a user-friendly interface to the OpenSSL toolkit. It provides graphical elements to specify the necessary parameters for OpenSSL, executes some sanity checks and shows feedback about the called OpenSSL functions.

6.7.1 Initialization

When initializing a certificate authority, a self-signed certificate must be created.

The default storage facility for cryptographic keys and certificates in Java Applications are so-called keystores[35].

The PGA CA uses the following parameters for creating such a self-signed certificate:

E-mail address is the address that is used as the distinguished name of the PGA CA.

Private key is the path to the file where the private key, generated during the initialization, should be stored.

---

[34] `http://www.jfree.org/jfreechart/`, last visited: January 2012

[35] `http://docs.oracle.com/javase/6/docs/technotes/tools/solaris/keytool.html#KeyStore`, last visited: January 2012

CA Certificate is the path to the file where the self-signed certificate of the CA, based on the private key, should be stored.

Truststore is the path to the key store file, where the self-signed certificate should be stored. This file can be used later when packaging all other PGA components to safely distribute the self-signed CA certificate.

Validity is the number of days the self-signed certificate is valid.

After checking that all parameters above are specified and valid, the PGA CA GUI calls OpenSSL to generate the self-signed certificate with several commands. The private key is generated with the following command:

```
openssl genrsa -out <privateKey> 1024
```

The parameter `genrsa` tells OpenSSL to generate an RSA [49] private key, the parameter `-out <privateKey>` tells OpenSSL to store the private key in the specified file (`<privateKey>` is the placeholder for the private key path specified by the user in the PGA CA GUI) and the parameter `1024` tells OpenSSL the size of the private key to generate in bits (the default value is only 512).

When the private key was successfully created, it is used to generate a certificate signing request. For that purpose a temporary OpenSSL configuration file with the following contents is created (`<email>` is the placeholder for the e-mail address specified by the user in the PGA CA GUI):

```
[ req ]
distinguished_name      = req_distinguished_name
prompt                  = no
[ req_distinguished_name ]
emailAddress            = <email>
```

This config file specifies that the given e-mail address is used as the distinguished name for the certificate request and it disables prompting the user at the command line (because in case of the PGA CA the command prompt is not visible to the user).

The certificate signing request is generated with the following command:

```
openssl req -new -config <configFileName>
        -key <privateKey> -out <requestFileName>
```

The parameter `req` tells OpenSSL to use its PKCS#10 [41] certificate request and certificate generating utility. The parameter `-new` tells OpenSSL to generate a new certificate request. The parameter `-config <configFileName>` specifies an alternative configuration file to override OpenSSL configuration values specified otherwise during compile time or in environment variables (`<configFileName>` is the placeholder for the temporary OpenSSL configuration file created above). The parameter `-key <privateKey>` tells OpenSSL to use the private key in the specified file for the certificate request (`<privateKey>` is again the placeholder for the private key path specified by the user in the PGA CA GUI). The parameter `-out <requestFileName>` tells OpenSSL to write the certificate request into the specified file. For this purpose, the PGA CA uses another temporary file.

The private key and the certificate request are both used to create the self-signed certificate. This is generated with the following command:

```
openssl x509 -req -days <days> -in <requestFileName>
        -signkey <privateKey> -out <certificateFileName>
```

The parameter `x509` tells OpenSSL to use its certificate display and signing utility. The parameter `-req` tells OpenSSL that it must handle a certificate request. The parameter `-days <days>` specifies the validity of the CA certificate to be generated (`<days>` is the placeholder for the CA certificate validity specified by the user in the PGA CA GUI). The parameter `-in <requestFileName>` specifies the name of the file to read the certificate request from (the temporary file used to create the certificate request above is just re-used here). The parameter `-signkey <privateKey>` supplies the private key used for self-signing the certificate (again, `<privateKey>` is the placeholder for the private key path specified by the user in the PGA CA GUI). The parameter `-out <certificateFileName>` tells OpenSSL to write the self-signed certificate into the specified file (`<certificateFileName>` is the placeholder for the CA certificate path specified by the user in the PGA CA GUI).

Finally, the Java security API (especially `java.security.KeyStore`, `java.security.cert.CertificateFactory`, `java.security.cert.Certificate` and `javax.net.ssl.TrustManagerFactory`) is used to store the self-signed certificate in the truststore specified by the user in the PGA CA GUI.

Some details of the CA certificate (issuer, subject and validity) are presented to the user in the graphical interface.

6.7.2 Certificate request handling

The PGA CA uses the following parameters for handling a certificate request:

Private key is the path to the file where the PGA CA private key is stored.

CA Certificate is the path to the file where the PGA CA self-signed certificate is stored.

Certificate request is the path to the file where the certificate request is stored.

Certificate is the path to the file where the issued certificate should be stored.

Validity is the number of days the issued certificate is valid.

After checking that all parameters above are specified and valid, the PGA CA GUI calls OpenSSL to process the certificate request with the following command:

```
openssl x509 -req -CAcreateserial -CA <certificateFileName>
        -CAkey <privateKey> -days <days>
        -in <requestFileName> -out <certificateFileName>
```

The parameter `x509` tells OpenSSL to use its certificate display and signing utility. The parameter `-req` tells OpenSSL that it must handle a certificate request. The parameter `-CAcreateserial` tells OpenSSL to create the CA serial number file if it does not exist. The parameter `-CA <certificateFileName>` specifies the certificate to be used for signing (`<certificateFileName>` is the placeholder for the CA certificate path specified by the user in the PGA CA GUI)). The parameter `-CAkey <privateKey>` specifies the CA private key to sign a certificate with (again, `<privateKey>` is the placeholder for the private key path specified by the user in the PGA CA GUI). The parameter `-days <days>` specifies the validity of the issued certificate to be generated (`<days>` is the placeholder for the certificate validity specified by the user in the PGA CA GUI). The parameter `-in <requestFileName>`

specifies the name of the file to read the certificate request from. The parameter `-out <certificateFileName>` tells OpenSSL to write the issued certificate into the specified file (`<certificateFileName>` is the placeholder for the issued certificate path specified by the user in the PGA CA GUI).

Identically to the CA certificate above, some details of the issued certificate (issuer, subject and validity) are presented to the user in the graphical interface.

6.7.3 Miscellaneous

The Java preferences system (esp. `java.util.prefs.Preferences`) is used to save all settings of the PGA CA GUI when the application exits. It is also used to restore all settings when the application is started.

Chapter 7

Usage

All PGA components are Java applications. Therefore they need an operating systems with an installed Java Virtual Machine.

7.1 Certificate Authority

The PGA CA is packaged as an executable JAR file (`pga_ca.jar`). On most systems it is sufficient to (double-)click the JAR file in a file browser or on the desktop to start the PGA CA. If this does not work or is not the preferred way to start the PGA CA, it can also be started via the command line with the following syntax:

```
java -jar pga_ca.jar
```

7.1.1 Initialization

The very first step when setting up a PGA infrastructure is to create the self-signed certificate. The graphical user interface of the PGA CA (see figure 7.1 on page 172) provides all elements to specify the necessary parameters for creating a self-signed certificate (for details see section 6.7.1 on page 166).

The validity of the generated self-signed CA certificate is shown in the certificate selection panel.

7.1.2 Certificate request handling

The graphical user interface of the PGA CA (see figure 7.2 on page 173) provides all elements to specify the necessary parameters for creating a self-signed certificate

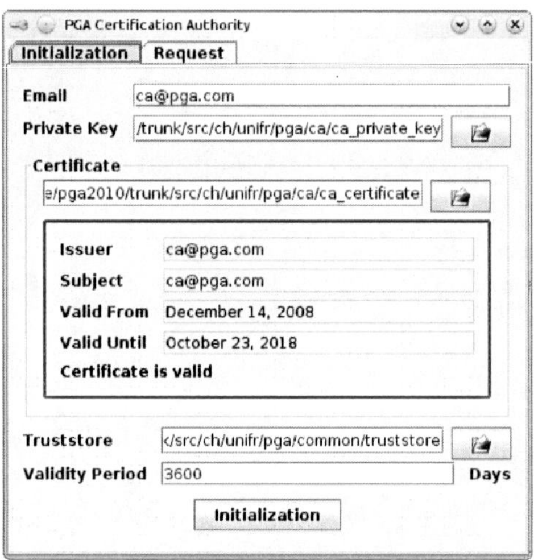

Figure 7.1: PGA CA initialization

(for details see section 6.7.2 on page 169). When a PGA Server operator sends a certificate signing request (via e-mail or other means), the PGA CA operator must select the request file, configure the file name of the issued certificate (probably based on the name of the currently handled PGA Server), configure the validity of the certificate and trigger the certificate creation process.

The validity of the issued certificate is shown in the certificate selection panel.

7.2 Server Core

The PGA Server Core is packaged as an executable JAR file (`pga_server_core.jar`). The PGA Server Core does not have a graphical user interface. Therefore the recommended way to start it is via the command line in a terminal. The PGA Server Core is remotely monitored and managed via JMX. This can require many different security options to ensure that unauthorized persons can not control or monitor the PGA Server Core. These options are described in detail in the JMX Documenta-

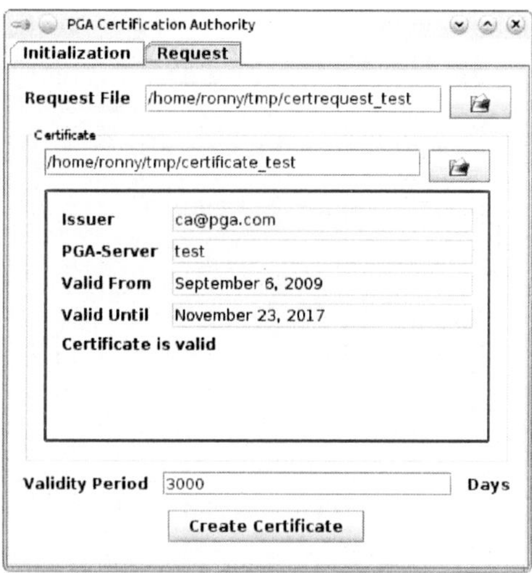

Figure 7.2: PGA CA request handling

tion[1].

The most simple configuration to start the PGA Server Core is with JMX without any authentication:

```
java -Djava.rmi.server.hostname=<hostname>
     -Dcom.sun.management.jmxremote.port=<port>
     -Dcom.sun.management.jmxremote.authenticate=false
     -Dcom.sun.management.jmxremote.ssl=false
     -jar pga_server_core.jar <--start>
```

The placeholder `<hostname>` must be replaced by the host name of the PGA Server Core, the placeholder `<port>` must be replaced by the port that should be used for the PGA Remote Management. In this configuration it is recommended to block access to this host and port for unauthorized persons by other means (e.g. by a firewall).

[1] `http://docs.oracle.com/javase/6/docs/technotes/guides/management/agent.html`, last visited: January 2012

Usually, the the anonymization service of the PGA Server Core is started by an operator of the graphical PGA Remote Management component. The parameter `--start` of the PGA Server Core application is optional and, if given, specifies that the anonymization service of the PGA Server Core should be started instantly instead. This is useful when the PGA Server Core is already fully configured and/or is started unattended (e.g. by system startup scripts).

7.3 Remote Management

The PGA Remote Management is packaged as a NetBeans module (`ch-unifr-pga-vvmplugin.nbm`). This module needs to be installed in the Java VisualVM. This is done by starting the Java VisualVM, opening the menu item `Tools` → `Plugins` (see fig. 7.3), selecting the tab `Downloaded`, pressing the button `Add Plugins...` and selecting and opening the file `ch-unifr-pga-vvmplugin.nbm` (see fig. 7.4).

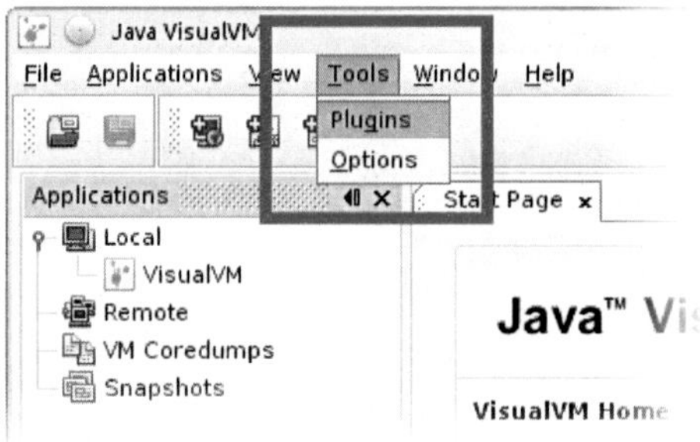

Figure 7.3: Java VisualVM Plugins

The Java Visual VM Plugins window displays the details about the PGA Remote Management module (version, author, date, source and description (see fig. 7.5). After checking the details, the `Install` button has to be pressed to start the Plugin Installer. The Plugin Installer first presents the list of all plugins to be installed (see fig. 7.6). After pressing the `Next` button, the license agreement of the PGA Remote Management will be displayed (see fig. 7.7). After accepting the terms of the license agreement the installation can be started by pressing the `Install` button.

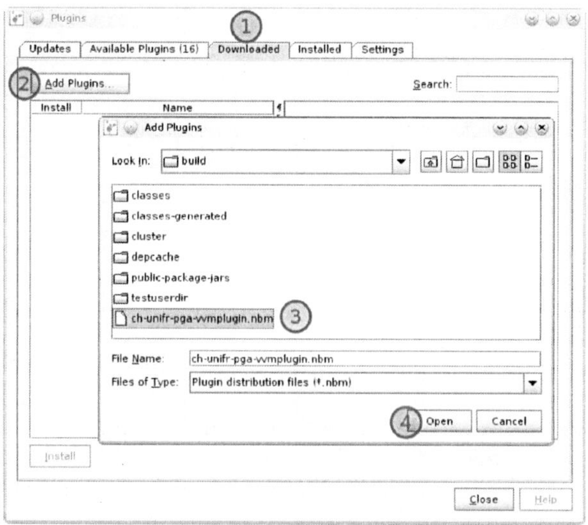

Figure 7.4: PGA Remote Management module selection

After installing the PGA Remote Management NetBeans module, the Java VirtualVM is able to manage all details of a PGA Server Core. When the PGA Server Core is running on the same host as the PGA Remote Management, the PGA Server Core appears in the Java VisualVM as a local process (see fig. 7.8).

When the PGA Server Core is running on a different host than the PGA Remote Management, a JMX connection must be added to the Java VisualVM by calling the menu item `File` → `Add JMX Connection...` (see fig. 7.9). The host name or IP address and the port of the remote application have to be specified, optional parameters are a display name for this JMX connection and, if configured, a username and password. The PGA Server Core then appears in the applications tree of the Java VisualVM under `Remote` → `<hostname>` → `<display name>` (see fig. 7.10).

The status area of the PGA Remote Management (see fig. 7.8) shows if the anonymization service is running or not, the number of currently connected PGA Clients, the remaining data volume for anonymous users and the currently configured list of anonymity groups. In addition to that it provides two buttons to start or stop the anonymization service.

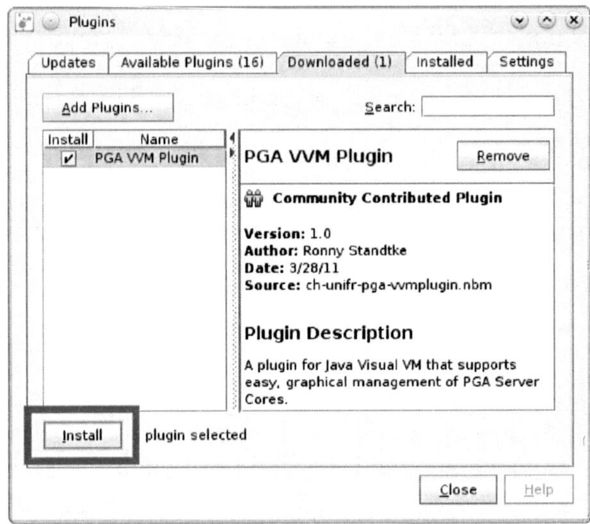

Figure 7.5: Added PGA Remote Management

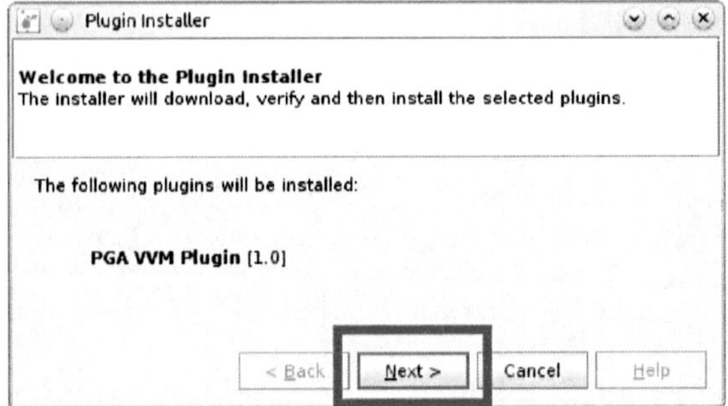

Figure 7.6: PGA Remote Management installation (1)

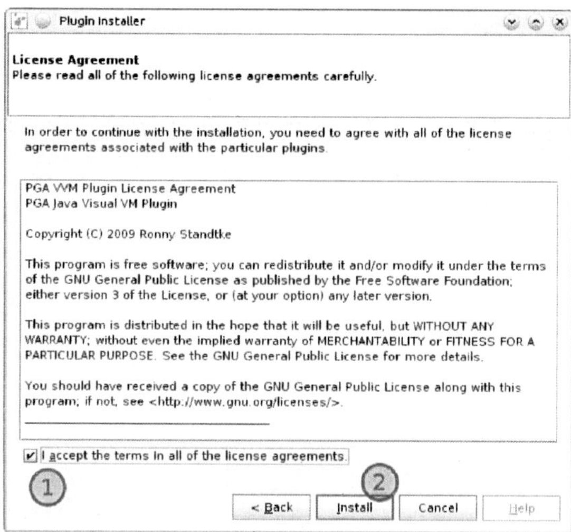

Figure 7.7: PGA Remote Management installation (2)

Figure 7.8: local PGA Server management

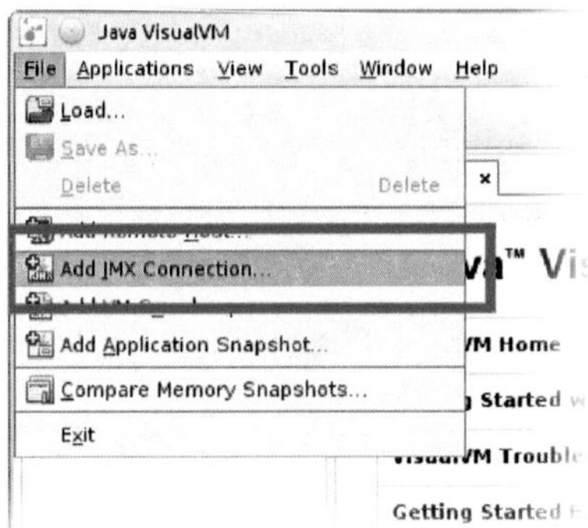

Figure 7.9: JMX connection with Java VisualVM

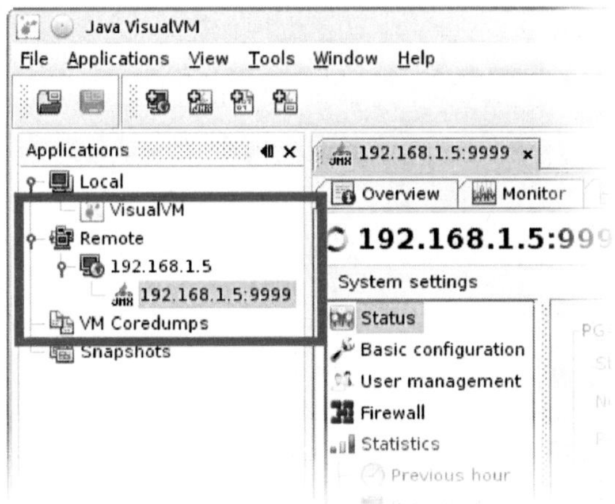

Figure 7.10: remote PGA Server management

In the basic configuration area of the PGA Remote Management (see fig. 7.11) the selected certificate file of the PGA Server Core, the anonymization service port, logging level, connection monitoring, log file rotation, monitoring filtering rules, encryption ID and the retention period are displayed and can be configured.

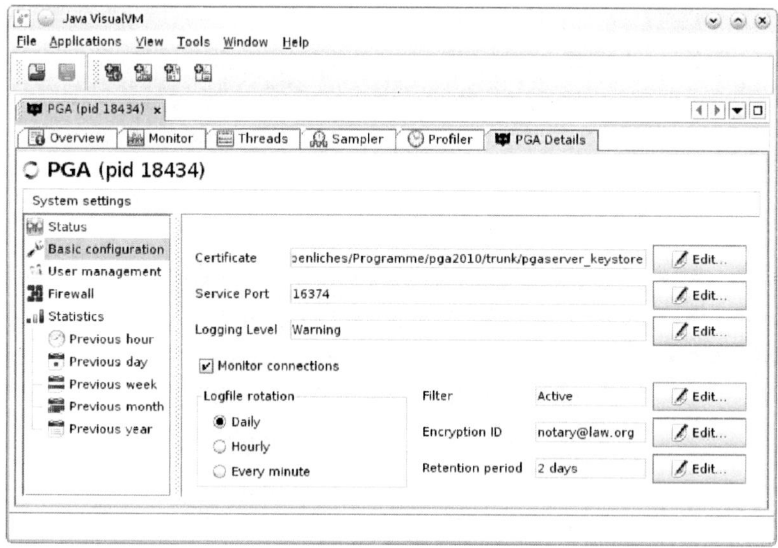

Figure 7.11: PGA Remote Management: Basic configuration

In the certificate configuration dialog (see fig. 7.12) a key pair for the PGA Server Core and a certificate request, e.g. for the PGA CA, can be generated and the issued certificate can be imported.

In the logging level configuration dialog (see fig. 7.13), the logging level for the PGA Server Core can be configured by pushing a slider to a certain level. An additional text field provides detailed information about each selected logging level.

In the monitoring filter dialog (see fig. 7.14), the regular expressions for filtering with target domains or IP addresses can be configured and tested.

In the user management area of the PGA Remote Management (see fig. 7.15) the available data volume and bandwidth for anonymous users and the available anonymity groups can be configured.

Figure 7.12: PGA Remote Management: Certificate configuration

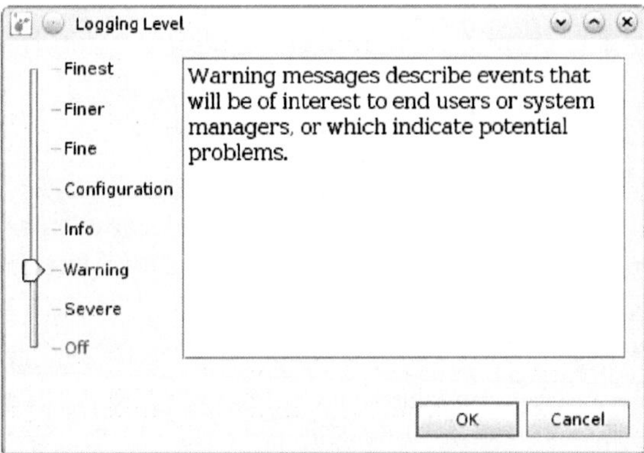

Figure 7.13: PGA Remote Management: Logging level configuration

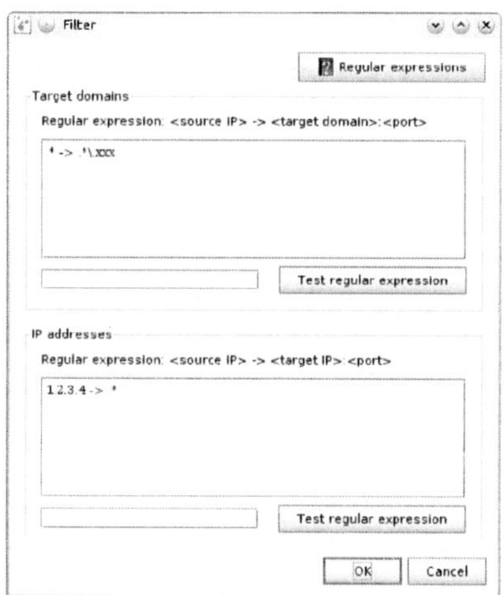

Figure 7.14: PGA Remote Management: Monitoring filter configuration

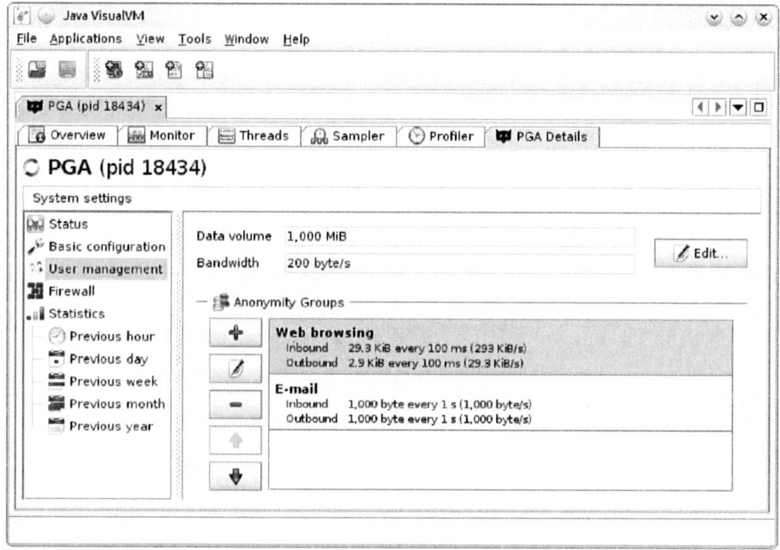

Figure 7.15: PGA Remote Management: User management

In the firewall area of the PGA Remote Management (see fig. 7.16) the list of internal networks can be configured and the set of firewall rules is displayed.

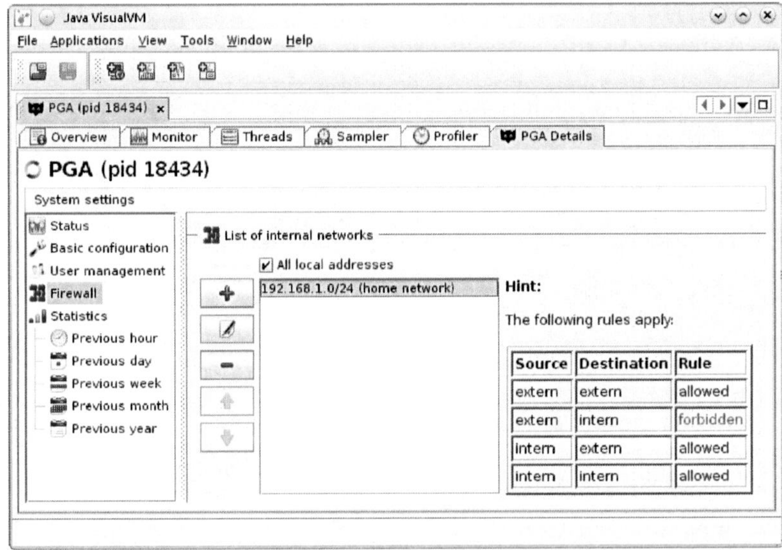

Figure 7.16: PGA Remote Management: Firewall

In the statistics area of the PGA Remote Management (see fig. 7.17) the statistics of used bandwidth, the number of PGA Clients, the CPU load and the Java VM memory can be shown and updated for the last hour, day, week, month and year.

7.4 Client

The PGA Client is packaged as an executable JAR file (`pga_client.jar`). On most systems it is sufficient to (double-)click the JAR file in a file browser or on the desktop to start the PGA Client. If this does not work or is not the preferred way to start the PGA Client, it can also be started via the command line with the following syntax:

```
java -jar pga_client.jar
```

Figure 7.17: PGA Remote Management: Statistics

When the PGA Client is started on a system for the very first time, a welcome dialog is opened (see fig. 7.18). There one can select if the PGA Client should start automatically when logging in or if it must be started manually. Automatically starting the PGA Client is recommended because this guarantees anonymization without gaps and starting the PGA Client can not be accidentally forgotten. The second setting in the welcome dialog is if the PGA Client should automatically connect to the last used PGA Server when starting up. Because most users will probably use one certain preferred PGA Server most of the time, this is a convenience setting for saving PGA Client users some mouse clicks at start-up.

Figure 7.18: PGA Client: Welcome dialog

After closing the welcome dialog the PGA Client shows the server selection panel (see fig. 7.19). There users can choose their preferred PGA Server to connect to. Selection can be done by either choosing from the combo box or by typing in the PGA Server address in the form:

```
<hostname>|<IP><:port>
```

A hostname or an IP address is mandatory. The port information is optional. If omitted, the default PGA Server port (`16374`) is used.

If the PGA Client is connected to a PGA Server, some details about the PGA Server (hostname or IP, monitoring status) is presented in the PGA Client main

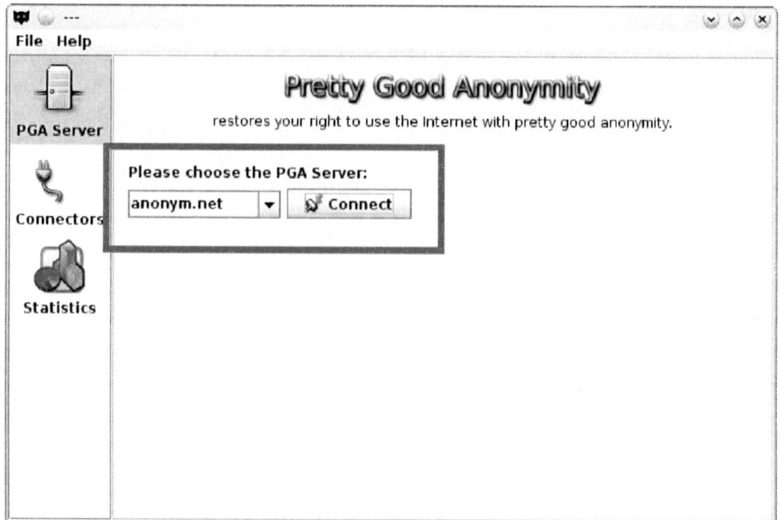

Figure 7.19: PGA Client: Server Selection

window (see fig. 7.19). More details about the connection to the selected PGA Server can be shown by clicking on the button `Details`. In this stage the user can join an anonymity group by pressing the button `Switch to High Security Mode`, open the manual about this subject by pressing the button `Why is this important?` and disconnect from the selected PGA Server by pressing the button `Disconnect from <PGA Server>` at the bottom of the main PGA Client window.

The details window (see fig. 7.21) shows on the left hand side graphs with the traffic history of the upstream and downstream traffic of the currently established tunnel to the selected PGA Server with details about data, dummy traffic and the overhead created by the used ciphers. On the right hand side it shows details about the selected PGA Server (system load, uptime, number of connected PGA Clients, reserved and remaining data volume for anonymous users, bandwidth for anonymous users, tunnel protocol, asymmetric cipher, symmetric cipher and the hash function).

When joining an anonymity group, the PGA Client first displays a list of known anonymity groups as specified by the operators of the selected PGA Server (see fig. 7.22). The properties of all anonymity groups are shown: package size and

Figure 7.20: PGA Client: Connected

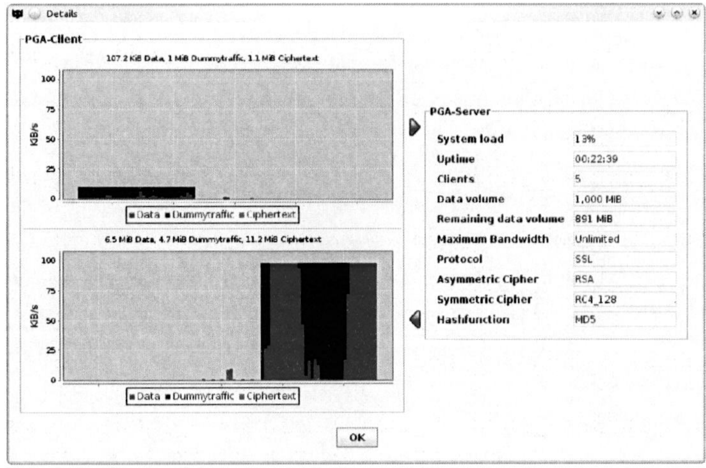

Figure 7.21: PGA Client: Details

sending frequency of both inbound and outbound streams and the current size of the anonymity group.

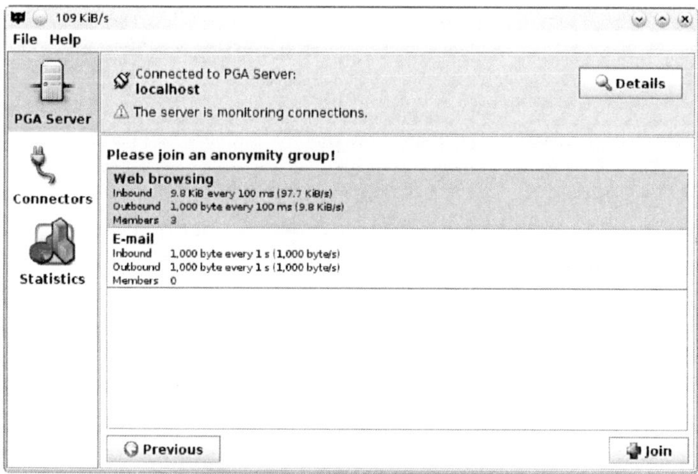

Figure 7.22: PGA Client: Anonymity groups list

After successfully joining an anonymity group, the PGA Client main window displays the currently selected anonymity group and provides a button to leave the anonymity group (see fig. 7.23).

On the left hand side of the PGA Client main window is a menu list with several menu items (`PGA Server`, `Connectors` and `Statistics`). When selecting the `Connectors` menu entry, the available PGA Client connector plugins are shown and can be configured in separate tabs. Currently, there are two connector plugins implemented: `Generic` and `Web Browser`. In the `Generic` connector plug-in tab one can configure the service port of the plug-in and start and stop the service (see fig. 7.24).

In the `Web Browser` connector plug-in tab (see fig. 7.25) one can open the relevant part of the PGA Client manual by pressing the `Direct Help...` button. The service port of the plug-in can be configured and the service can be started and stopped. At the bottom of the plug-in tab some statistics about web browser connections and HTTP requests are displayed.

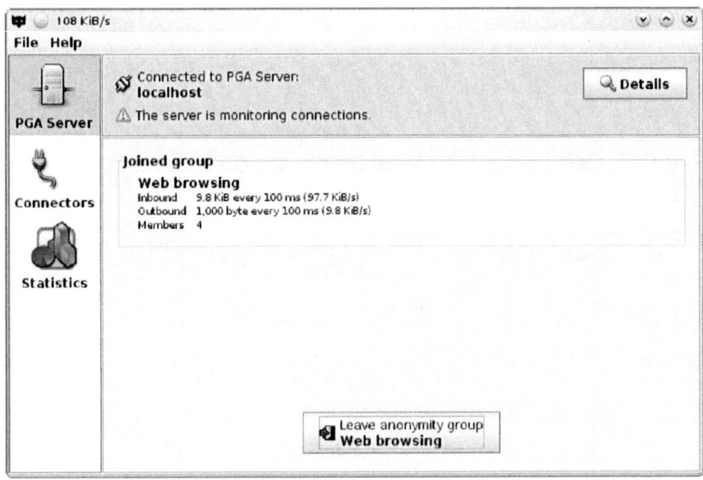

Figure 7.23: PGA Client: Joined an anonymity group

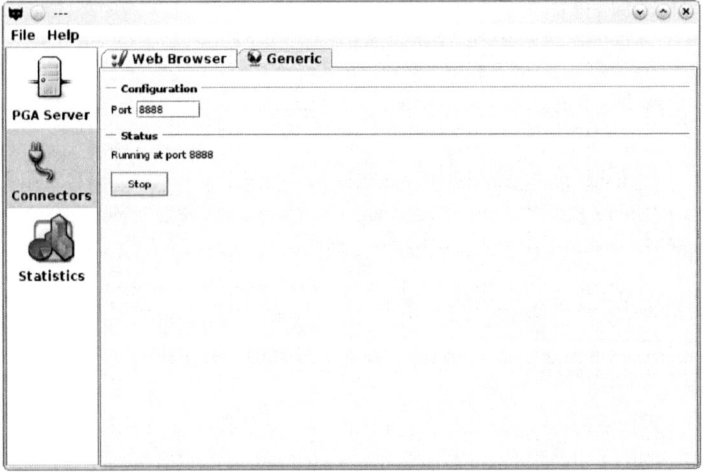

Figure 7.24: PGA Client: Generic connector

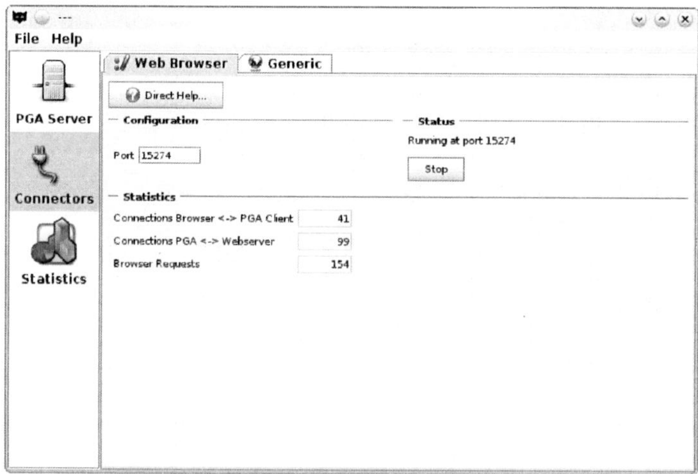

Figure 7.25: PGA Client: Web Browser connector

When selecting the `Statistics` entry in the PGA Client window main menu (see fig. 7.26), some details about the upstream, downstream and total traffic generated and consumed by the PGA Client are displayed.

The settings dialog of the PGA Client can be opened by selecting the menu item `File` → `Settings...`. It has a menu list at the left hand sides that provides access to three different settings areas: `Start`, `Ciphers` and `Logging Level`. When selecting the `Start` menu entry (see fig. 7.27), the start-up behavior of the PGA Client can be configured (see page 184 for details).

When selecting the `Ciphers` menu entry (see fig. 7.28), the ciphers which are used to establish the tunnel to the PGA Server can be configured. Either the default ciphers can be used (all supported ciphers) or the enabled ciphers can be manually selected from the list of supported ciphers.

When selecting the `Logging Level` menu entry (see fig. 7.29), the logging level for the PGA Client can be configured by pushing a slider to a certain level. An additional text field provides detailed information about each selected logging level.

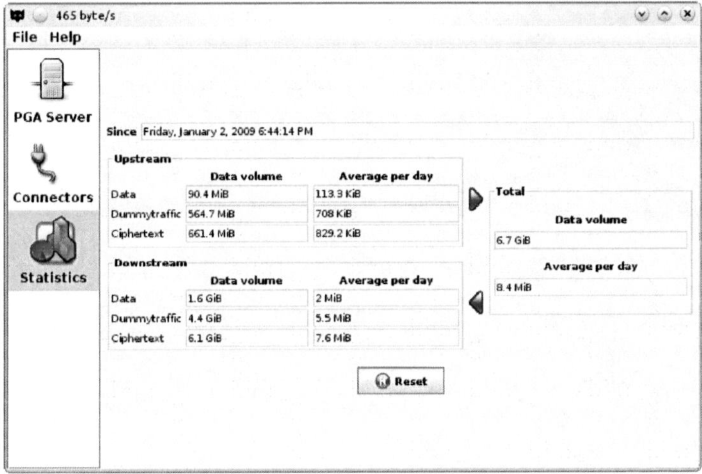

Figure 7.26: PGA Client: Statistics

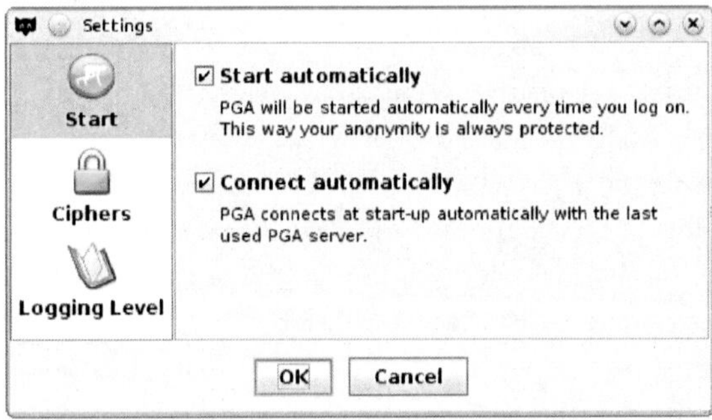

Figure 7.27: PGA Client: Start settings

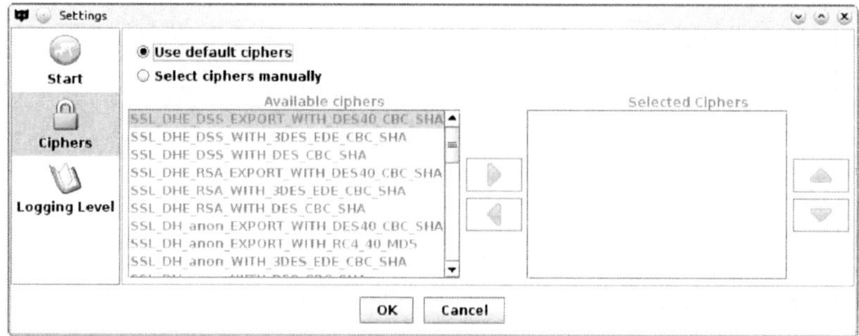

Figure 7.28: PGA Client: Cipher settings

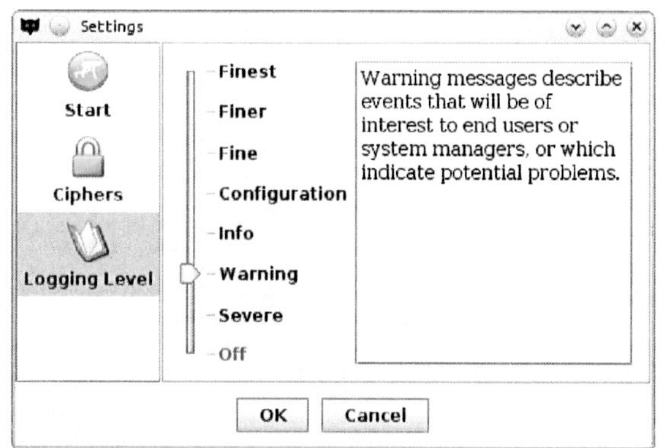

Figure 7.29: PGA Client: Logging level settings

Chapter 8

Conclusion

The lack of a simple and secure implementation of anonymization via anonymity groups was the motivation of this work. The goal of this thesis was to design and implement such an architecture that provides flexible, high-bandwidth and low-latency anonymous Internet communication that provides a high level of security against global adversaries with a low level of complexity.

In order to do that, first of all, the already existing solutions have been evaluated. The security mechanisms that protect against a global attacker (message collection, reordering and transcoding) have been reused. The evaluation has shown that mechanisms of existing solutions that try to also protect against the anonymity provider itself (distribution of the anonymity provider) are not very effective as there are still many sophisticated and successful attacks against such mechanisms. Therefore, these complex mechanisms have been left out in favor of high-performance and low complexity.

To create large anonymity groups (one significant property of good anonymization) it became necessary in the course of implementing the architecture of this thesis, to design and implement a scalable, flexible and easy-to-use framework for high-performance, low-latency and secure I/O processing: the Java NIO Framework. This framework implements readiness selection in Java with a good utilization of multi-core and many-core processing units. The Java NIO Framework has been published as Free Software released under the GNU Lesser General Public License. It has been presented on ICSOFT 2008, the 3th International Conference on Software and Data Technologies [57], was reviewed by other universities and is now in use not only for the architecture of this thesis but also in computing clusters with more than 1000 nodes.

Several software components for the anonymization architecture have been designed and implemented:

- an easy-to-use, platform and application independent client
- a high-performance, scalable, secure and remotely manageable server
- an easy-to-use remote management solution for the server component
- a simple certificate authority to provide authentication for the anonymization architecture
- several new protocols to provide efficient and application independent anonymization of already existing Internet communication

There are several aspects of the solution provided in this thesis that can be improved by future works:

- The current design of the certificate authority is very simple and omits several building blocks of complete certificate solutions like Certificate Revocation Lists or CA certificate updates.
- The current implementation of the server component lacks user management and user defined anonymity groups.
- The filtering rules of the logging component can currently not be based on source domains.
- The HTTP proxy of the client component currently only supports a subset of HTTP.
- Only telnet and HTTP are the currently supported protocols. Other protocols could be implemented at a later stage.

Appendix A

ProMeLa models

A.1 Message tunneling

```
mtype = {OPEN, OPEN_FAILED, OPEN_SUCCEEDED, DATA, SHUTDOWN, ERROR};

chan server_to_client = [10] of {mtype};
chan client_to_server = [10] of {mtype};

active proctype PGA_Client()
{
INITIAL:        client_to_server!OPEN;
WAITING:        if
                :: server_to_client?OPEN_FAILED -> goto TERMINAL
                :: server_to_client?OPEN_SUCCEEDED
                fi;

ESTABLISHED:    do
                :: client_to_server!DATA
                :: client_to_server!SHUTDOWN -> goto WRITE_ONLY
                :: client_to_server!ERROR    -> goto TERMINAL
                :: server_to_client?DATA
                :: server_to_client?SHUTDOWN -> goto READ_ONLY
                :: server_to_client?ERROR ->
                   client_to_server!SHUTDOWN; goto TERMINAL
```

```
                od;

READ_ONLY:      do
                :: client_to_server!DATA
                :: client_to_server!SHUTDOWN -> goto TERMINAL
                :: client_to_server!ERROR    -> goto TERMINAL
                :: server_to_client?ERROR ->
                    client_to_server!SHUTDOWN; goto TERMINAL
                od;

WRITE_ONLY:     do
                :: client_to_server!ERROR    -> goto TERMINAL
                :: server_to_client?DATA
                :: server_to_client?SHUTDOWN -> goto TERMINAL
                :: server_to_client?ERROR    -> goto TERMINAL
                od;

TERMINAL:       printf("PGA Client reached TERMINAL state \n")
}


active proctype PGA_Server_Core()
{
INITIAL:        client_to_server?OPEN;
WAITING:        if
                :: server_to_client!OPEN_FAILED -> goto TERMINAL
                :: server_to_client!OPEN_SUCCEEDED
                fi;

ESTABLISHED:    do
                :: server_to_client!DATA
                :: server_to_client!SHUTDOWN -> goto WRITE_ONLY
                :: server_to_client!ERROR    -> goto PENDING
                :: client_to_server?DATA
```

```
                    :: client_to_server?SHUTDOWN -> goto READ_ONLY
                    :: client_to_server?ERROR    -> goto TERMINAL
                    od;

READ_ONLY:          do
                    :: server_to_client!DATA
                    :: server_to_client!SHUTDOWN -> goto TERMINAL
                    :: server_to_client!ERROR    -> goto TERMINAL
                    :: client_to_server?ERROR    -> goto TERMINAL
                    od;

WRITE_ONLY:         do
                    :: server_to_client!ERROR    -> goto PENDING
                    :: client_to_server?DATA
                    :: client_to_server?SHUTDOWN -> goto TERMINAL
                    :: client_to_server?ERROR    -> goto TERMINAL
                    od;

PENDING:            do
                    :: client_to_server?DATA
                    :: client_to_server?SHUTDOWN -> goto TERMINAL
                    :: client_to_server?ERROR    -> goto TERMINAL
                    od;

TERMINAL:           printf("PGA Server reached TERMINAL state \n")
}
```

A.2 XON/XOFF flow control

```
mtype = {DATA, XON, XOFF}

init {
    chan server_to_client = [3] of {mtype};
    chan client_to_server = [3] of {mtype};
```

```
    run PGA_Component(server_to_client, client_to_server);
    run PGA_Component(client_to_server, server_to_client);
}

proctype PGA_Component(chan readChannel; chan writeChannel) {
ON_ON:          do
                :: writeChannel!DATA
                :: readChannel?DATA ->
                     if
                     :: writeChannel!XOFF -> goto ON_OFF
                     :: skip
                     fi
                :: readChannel?XOFF -> goto OFF_ON
                od;

ON_OFF:         do
                :: writeChannel!DATA
                :: writeChannel!XON -> goto ON_ON
                :: readChannel?DATA ->
                    if
                    :: goto ON_E
                    :: skip
                    fi
                :: readChannel?XOFF -> goto OFF_OFF
                od;

ON_E:           do
                :: writeChannel!DATA
                :: goto ON_OFF
                :: writeChannel!XON -> goto ON_ON
                od;

OFF_ON:         do
                :: readChannel?DATA ->
```

```
                    if
                    :: writeChannel!XOFF -> goto OFF_OFF
                    :: skip
                    fi
                :: readChannel?XON -> goto ON_ON
                od;

OFF_OFF:        do
                :: writeChannel!XON -> goto OFF_ON
                :: readChannel?DATA ->
                    if
                    :: goto OFF_E
                    :: skip
                    fi
                :: readChannel?XON -> goto ON_OFF
                od;

OFF_E:          do
                :: goto OFF_OFF
                :: writeChannel!XON -> goto OFF_ON
                od;
}
```

Bibliography

[1] ANSI: *US-ASCII. Coded Character Set - 7-Bit American Standard Code for Information Interchange. Standard ANSI X3.4-1986.* 1986

[2] ARCAND, Jean-Francois: *Project Grizzly.* https://grizzly.dev.java.net. Version: 2006

[3] BARRETT, Daniel J. ; SILVERMAN, Richard E.: *SSH, The Secure Shell: The Definitive Guide.* Sebastopol, CA, USA : O'Reilly & Associates, Inc., 2001. – ISBN 0596000111

[4] BECK, Kent ; BEEDLE, Mike ; BENNEKUM, Arie van ; COCKBURN, Alistair ; CUNNINGHAM, Ward ; FOWLER, Martin ; GRENNING, James ; HIGHSMITH, Jim ; HUNT, Andrew ; JEFFRIES, Ron ; KERN, Jon ; MARICK, Brian ; MARTIN, Robert C. ; MELLOR, Steve ; SCHWABER, Ken ; SUTHERLAND, Jeff ; THOMAS, Dave: *Manifesto for Agile Software Development.* http://www.agilemanifesto.org/. Version: 2001

[5] BERTHOLD, Oliver ; FEDERRATH, Hannes ; KÖPSELL, Stefan: Web MIXes: A system for anonymous and unobservable Internet access. In: FEDERRATH, H. (Hrsg.): *Proceedings of Designing Privacy Enhancing Technologies: Workshop on Design Issues in Anonymity and Unobservability,* Springer-Verlag, LNCS 2009, July 2000, S. 115–129

[6] BLOCH, Joshua: *Effective Java programming language guide.* Mountain View, CA, USA : Sun Microsystems, Inc., 2001. – ISBN 0–201–31005–8

[7] BOEHM, Barry W.: A Spiral Model of Software Development and Enhancement. In: *Computer* 21 (1988), S. 61–72. http://dx.doi.org/http://doi.ieeecomputersociety.org/10.1109/2.59. – DOI http://doi.ieeecomputersociety.org/10.1109/2.59. – ISSN 0018–9162

[8] BRAY, Tim ; PAOLI, Jean ; SPERBERG-MCQUEEN, C. M. ; MALER, Eve ; YERGEAU, François: *Extensible Markup Language (XML) 1.0 (Fifth Edition)*. World Wide Web Consortium, Recommendation REC-xml-20081126. http://www.w3.org/TR/2008/REC-xml-20081126. Version: November 2008

[9] CERF, V. G. ; KAHN, R.: A protocol for packet network intercommunication. (1988), S. 10–21. ISBN 0–89006–337–0

[10] CHAUM, David: Untraceable electronic mail, return addresses, and digital pseudonyms. In: *Communications of the ACM* 24 (1981), February, Nr. 2

[11] CHAUM, David: Blind Signatures for Untraceable Payments. In: *CRYPTO*, 1982, S. 199–203

[12] CHAUM, David ; FIAT, Amos ; NAOR, Moni: Untraceable Electronic Cash. In: *CRYPTO*, 1988, S. 319–327

[13] COHEN, Danny: On Holy Wars and a Plea for Peace. In: *Computer* 14 (1981), S. 48–54. http://dx.doi.org/http://doi.ieeecomputersociety.org/10.1109/C-M.1981.220208. – DOI http://doi.ieeecomputersociety.org/10.1109/C–M.1981.220208. – ISSN 0018–9162

[14] COOPER, D. ; SANTESSON, S. ; FARRELL, S. ; BOEYEN, S. ; HOUSLEY, R. ; POLK, W.: RFC 5280 - Internet X.509 Public Key Infrastructure Certificate and Certificate Revocation List (CRL) Profile. Version: May 2008. http://tools.ietf.org/html/rfc5280. 2008. – Forschungsbericht

[15] DINGLEDINE, Roger ; MATHEWSON, Nick ; SYVERSON, Paul: Tor: The Second-Generation Onion Router. In: *Proceedings of the 13th USENIX Security Symposium*, 2004

[16] EUROPEAN PARLIAMENT AND THE COUNCIL: *Directive 2006/24/EC of the European Parliament and of the Council of 15 March 2006 on the retention of data generated or processed in connection with the provision of publicly available electronic communications services or of public communications networks and amending Directive 2002/58/EC*. http://eur-lex.europa.eu/LexUriServ/LexUriServ.do?uri=CELEX:32006L0024:EN:HTML

[17] FIELDING, R. ; GETTYS, J. ; MOGUL, J. ; FRYSTYK, H. ; MASINTER, L. ; LEACH, P. ; BERNERS-LEE, T.: *Hypertext Transfer Protocol - HTTP/1.1.* United States, 1999

[18] FIELDING, R. ; GETTYS, J. ; MOGUL, J. ; FRYSTYK, H. ; MASINTER, L. ; LEACH, P. ; BERNERS-LEE, T.: *RFC 2616, Hypertext Transfer Protocol – HTTP/1.1.* `http://www.rfc.net/rfc2616.html`. Version: 1999

[19] FISK, Mike ; FENG, Wu chun: Dynamic Adjustment of TCP Window Sizes / Tech. Rep. Los Alamos Unclassified Report (LAUR) 00-3221, Los Alamos National Laboratory. 2000. – Forschungsbericht

[20] FORMAN, Ira R. ; FORMAN, Nate: *Java Reflection in Action (In Action series).* Greenwich, CT, USA : Manning Publications Co., 2004. – ISBN 1932394184

[21] FREEDMAN, Michael J. ; MORRIS, Robert: Tarzan: A Peer-to-Peer Anonymizing Network Layer. In: *Proceedings of the 9th ACM Conference on Computer and Communications Security (CCS 2002).* Washington, DC, November 2002

[22] GAMMA, Erich ; HELM, Richard ; JOHNSON, Ralph ; VLISSIDES, John: *Design Patterns.* Boston, MA : Addison-Wesley, 1995. – ISBN 0201633612

[23] GOLDSCHLAG, David M. ; REED, Michael G. ; SYVERSON, Paul F.: Hiding Routing Information. In: ANDERSON, R. (Hrsg.): *Proceedings of Information Hiding: First International Workshop*, Springer-Verlag, LNCS 1174, May 1996, S. 137–150

[24] GOSLING, James ; JOY, Bill ; STEELE, Guy ; BRACHA, Gilad: *Java(TM) Language Specification, The (3rd Edition) (Java (Addison-Wesley)).* Addison-Wesley Professional, 2005. – ISBN 0321246780

[25] HITCHENS, Ron: *Java NIO.* O'Reilly & Associates, Inc., 2002

[26] HITCHENS, Ron: How to Build a Scalable Multiplexed Server With NIO JavaOne Conference, 2006

[27] HOARE, C. A. R.: Quicksort. In: *Computer Journal* 5 (1962), April, Nr. 1, S. 10–15

[28] HOLZMANN, Gerard J.: *The SPIN Model Checker: Primer and Reference Manual*. Addison-Wesley Professional, 2003. – ISBN 0321228626

[29] HOY, Marc ; WOOD, Dave ; LOY, Marc ; ELLIOT, James ; ECKSTEIN, Robert: *Java Swing*. Sebastopol, CA, USA : O'Reilly & Associates, Inc., 2002. – ISBN 0596004087

[30] IEEE ITU-T: *Recommendation G.114. One-Way Transmission Time*. `http://www.itu.int/rec/dologin_pub.asp?lang=e&id=T-REC-G.114-200305-I!!PDF-E&type=items`. Version: 2009

[31] INFORMATION SCIENCES INSTITUTE, UNIVERSITY OF SOUTHERN CALIFORNIA: *RFC 793, Transmission Control Protocol*. `http://tools.ietf.org/html/rfc0793`. Version: 1981

[32] JAMES O. COPLIEN, Douglas C. S.: *Pattern Languages of Program Design*. Addison-Wesley, 1995

[33] KESDOGAN, Dogan ; EGNER, Jan ; BÜSCHKES, Roland: Stop-and-Go MIXes: Providing Probabilistic Anonymity in an Open System. In: *Proceedings of Information Hiding Workshop (IH 1998)*, Springer-Verlag, LNCS 1525, 1998

[34] KNUTH, Donald E.: Backus Normal Form vs. Backus Naur Form. In: *Commun. ACM* 7 (1964), Nr. 12, S. 735–736. `http://dx.doi.org/http://doi.acm.org/10.1145/355588.365140`. – DOI http://doi.acm.org/10.1145/355588.365140. – ISSN 0001–0782

[35] LARMAN, Craig ; BASILI, Victor R.: Iterative and Incremental Development: A Brief History. In: *Computer* 36 (2003), S. 47–56. `http://dx.doi.org/http://doi.ieeecomputersociety.org/10.1109/MC.2003.1204375`. – DOI http://doi.ieeecomputersociety.org/10.1109/MC.2003.1204375. – ISSN 0018–9162

[36] LEE, Trustin: *Apache MINA Project*. `http://mina.apache.org`. Version: 2006

[37] LINDHOLM, Tim ; YELLIN, Frank: *Java Virtual Machine Specification*. Boston, MA, USA : Addison-Wesley Longman Publishing Co., Inc., 1999. – ISBN 0201432943

[38] MAIWALD, Eric: *Network Security: A Beginner's Guide.* McGraw-Hill Professional, 2001. – ISBN 0072133244

[39] MOORE, Gordon E.: Cramming more components onto integrated circuits. In: *Electronics* 38 (1965), April, Nr. 8

[40] MURDOCH, Steven J. ; DANEZIS, George: Low-Cost Traffic Analysis of Tor. In: *Proceedings of the 2005 IEEE Symposium on Security and Privacy*, IEEE CS, May 2005

[41] NYSTROM, M. ; KALISKI, B.: *PKCS #10: Certification Request Syntax Specification Version 1.7.* United States, 2000

[42] PAREKH, Sameer: Prospects for Remailers. In: *First Monday* 1 (1996), August, Nr. 2

[43] PEIERLS, Tim ; GOETZ, Brian ; BLOCH, Joshua ; BOWBEER, Joseph ; LEA, Doug ; HOLMES, David: *Java Concurrency in Practice.* Addison-Wesley Professional, 2005. – ISBN 0321349601

[44] PERRY, J. S. ; DENN, Robert (Hrsg.): *Java Management Extensions.* 1st. Sebastopol, CA, USA : O'Reilly & Associates, Inc., 2002. – ISBN 0596002459

[45] PITT, Esmond: *Fundamental Networking in Java.* Secaucus, NJ, USA : Springer-Verlag New York, Inc., 2005. – ISBN 1846280303

[46] REED, Michael G. ; SYVERSON, Paul F. ; GOLDSCHLAG, David M.: Anonymous Connections and Onion Routing. In: *IEEE Journal on Selected Areas in Communications* 16 (1998), S. 482–494

[47] REKHTER, Y. ; LI, T.: *An Architecture for IP Address Allocation with CIDR.* United States, 1993

[48] RENNHARD, Marc ; PLATTNER, Bernhard: Practical Anonymity for the Masses with MorphMix. In: JUELS, Ari (Hrsg.): *Proceedings of Financial Cryptography (FC '04)*, Springer-Verlag, LNCS 3110, February 2004, S. 233–250

[49] RIVEST, R. L. ; SHAMIR, A. ; ADLEMAN, L.: A method for obtaining digital signatures and public-key cryptosystems. In: *Commun. ACM* 21 (1978),

February, 120–126. http://doi.acm.org/10.1145/359340.359342. – ISSN 0001–0782

[50] ROBERT, Tim Berners-Lee ; CAILLIAU, Robert ; POLLERMANN, Bernd: World-Wide Web: The Information Universe. In: *Communications of the ACM* 37 (1992), S. 76–82

[51] ROTH, Gregor: *xSocket*. http://xsocket.sourceforge.net. Version: 2006

[52] ROYCE, W. W.: Managing the development of large software systems: concepts and techniques. In: *ICSE '87: Proceedings of the 9th international conference on Software Engineering*. Los Alamitos, CA, USA : IEEE Computer Society Press, 1987. – ISBN 0–89791–216–0, S. 328–338

[53] RSS ADVISORY BOARD: *Really Simple Syndication (RSS)*. http://www.rssboard.org/rss-specification, 2009

[54] SAILER, Reiner ; FEDERRATH, Hannes ; PFITZMANN, Andreas: *Security Functions in Telecommunications - Placement Achievable Security*. 1999

[55] SHETTY, Akshathkumar: *QuickServer*. http://www.quickserver.org. Version: 2006

[56] STANDTKE, Ronny ; ULTES-NITSCHE, Ulrich: Pretty Good Anonymity. In: *Proceedings of KiVs 2007, Kommunikation in Verteilten Systemen, 15. ITG/GI-Fachtagung, Bern*, VDE Verlag, 2007

[57] STANDTKE, Ronny ; ULTES-NITSCHE, Ulrich: Java NIO Framework. In: *Proceedings of Third International Conference on Software and Data Technologies*, INSTICC Press, 2008

[58] SYVERSON, Paul ; REED, Michael ; GOLDSCHLAG, David: Onion Routing Access Configurations. In: *Proceedings of the DARPA Information Survivability Conference and Exposition (DISCEX 2000)* Bd. 1, IEEE CS Press, 2000, S. 34–40

[59] SYVERSON, Paul ; TSUDIK, Gene ; REED, Michael ; LANDWEHR, Carl: Towards an Analysis of Onion Routing Security. In: FEDERRATH, H. (Hrsg.):

Proceedings of Designing Privacy Enhancing Technologies: Workshop on Design Issues in Anonymity and Unobservability, Springer-Verlag, LNCS 2009, July 2000, S. 96–114

[60] TANENBAUM, Andrew: *Computer Networks.* Prentice Hall Professional Technical Reference, 2002. – ISBN 0130661023

[61] THE IEEE AND THE OPEN GROUP: *The Open Group Base Specifications Issue 7, IEEE Std 1003.1-2008.* http://www.opengroup.org/onlinepubs/9699919799/utilities/at.html, 2008

[62] THE IEEE AND THE OPEN GROUP: *The Open Group Base Specifications Issue 7, IEEE Std 1003.1-2008.* http://www.opengroup.org/onlinepubs/9699919799/utilities/crontab.html, 2008

[63] TURING, Alan M.: On Computable Numbers, with an Application to the Entscheidungsproblem. In: *Proceedings of the London Mathematical Society* 2 (1936), Nr. 42, 230–265. `http://www.cs.helsinki.fi/u/gionis/cc05/OnComputableNumbers.pdf`

[64] UT, Bo ; FREIER, Attn A. ; FREIER, Alan O. ; KOCHER, Paul C. ; KARLTON, Philip L. ; ABADI, Martin ; RELYEA, Robert ; ELGAMAL, Taher ; ROSKIND, Jim ; GANGOLLI, Anil ; SABIN, Micheal J. ; D, Ph. ; WEINSTEIN, Tom ; BALDWIN, Robert ; MONMA, Clyde ; COX, George ; MURRAY, Eric ; DOWELL, Cheri ; RUBIN, Avi: *SSL Version 3.0 3/4/96 56 Send all written communication about*

[65] VIEGA, John ; MESSIER, Matt ; CHANDRA, Pravir: *Network Security with OpenSSL: Cryptography for Secure Communications.* O'Reilly Media, 2002 `http://www.worldcat.org/isbn/059600270X`. – ISBN 059600270X